# The Ultimate Lean and Green Cookbook for Beginners 2021

1000 Days Fueling Hacks & Lean and Green Recipes to Help You Keep Healthy and Lose Weight by Harnessing the Power of "Fueling Hacks Meals"

**Mitch Sams**

# Table of Contents

# Introduction

## What is the Lean & Green Meal?

The standard Lean & Green meal diet usually comprises 5 – 7 ounces of lean proteins (cooked), 2 servings of healthy fats, and around 3 servings of non-starchy veggies. The diet plan allows you to have your Lean & Green meals at any of the six meal slots devised throughout the day. Moreover, you can adjust your meal timings according to your schedule.

## Substitution of Fueling for Lean & Green Meals

There are two significant reasons why Fueling should not be considered as a substitute for Lean & Green meals. They are as follows:

1. The Lean & Green meals are a great source of proteins, healthy fats, essential calories, fiber, and various other healthy nutrients. They are considerably different from the nutritional properties of the Fuelings. For example, the required quantity of healthy fats is not sufficiently provided by Fuelings. Instead, the Lean & Green meals are the primary and befitting source to cater for the nutritional fat demands of the body. Moreover, Lean & Green meals are beneficial in establishing a more balanced approach between all the nutrients like proteins,

carbs, and essential calories. Additionally, it also effective in the promotion of a mild fat-burning process, and making you feel fuller, and lets you have lesser food cravings.

2. Furthermore, they are also very effective in imparting healthy habits like making nourishing, healthy, and nutritious meals. It serves the true essence of lean & green, i.e., "Lifelong Transformation, One Healthy Habitat A Time".

## Managing Meals

To achieve the most out of your diet plan, it is crucial to consume all of your Lean & Green meals and the Fuelings every day. Failing to do so clearly leads to a lesser intake of essential minerals, vitamins, protein, and calories, causing hindrance in the success of the diet plan.

## Missed a Fueling? Here's what to Do

Having all your Lean & Green meals and Fuelings in the right portions at the correct times is very important for a successful diet plan. In case you miss a specific meal, you have to manage your meals a bit close together to ensure that you get all your meals at the end of the day.

It is essential to understand that skipping meals won't enhance your weight loss; in fact, it might be the opposite. If you want to decide between "doubling" or "skipping" a meal, we recommend "doubling up" your meals, i.e., to have two Fuelings together, and ensure that you get all your necessary Lean & Green meals and Fuelings at the end of the day.

## Maintaining Heating Habits

The Lean & Green diet plan ensures that you consume healthy meals six times a day, i.e., one meal after every 2 – 3 hours. You can make a schedule of your meal times according to your own requirements and follow it thoroughly according to the guidelines of six meals per day, i.e., both Lean & Green meals & Fuelings throughout the 24 hours timespan.

We recommend having your first meal in the first hour of waking up, then have another one after a 2 – 3 to maintain optimal hunger control and blood sugar. You can adjust your eating routine on weekends to cater for your daily routine effectively.

# Part Ⅰ Lean and Green Recipes

# Breakfast Recipes

## Cheddar Broccoli Bread

**Preparation Time:** 15 minutes
**Cooking Time:** 45 minutes
**Servings:** 3

**Ingredients:**

- ¼ cup shredded reduced-fat cheddar
- 3 cups small broccoli florets
- 1/8 teaspoon cayenne pepper
- 4 eggs
- 1/8 teaspoon black pepper
- ½ cup unsweetened almond milk
- Salt, to taste

**Preparation:**

1. Preheat the oven to 375 degrees F.
2. Add 2 tablespoons water and broccoli in a microwave safe bowl and microwave it for about 4 minutes.
3. Take out and strain the broccoli.
4. Meanwhile, add black pepper, cayenne pepper, salt, eggs, and almond milk in a large bowl. Beat well.
5. In a greased baking dish, arrange broccoli in the bottom and sprinkle cheese on it.
6. Pour the egg mixture on broccoli and cheese and bake for about 45 minutes.
7. Take out, slice, and serve.

**Serving Suggestions:** Serve with tea.

**Variation Tip:** You can also use mozzarella cheese for an even better taste.

**Nutritional Information per Serving:**

**Calories:** 653 | **Fat:** 36.9g|**Sat Fat:** 2.2g|**Carbohydrates:** 24g|**Fiber:** 9.2g|**Sugar:** 0.5g|**Protein:** 57.2g

# Egg Muffin

**Preparation Time:** 10 minutes
**Cooking Time:** 20 minutes
**Servings:** 3

**Ingredients:**

- 4 eggs
- 6 tablespoons low-fat Greek yogurt
- ½ cup liquid egg whites
- Salt, to taste

**Preparation:**

1. Warm up the baking oven to 375 degrees F.
2. Meanwhile, add eggs, yogurt, egg whites and salt in a bowl. Whisk well.
3. Pour this mixture in greased muffin tins and put them in baking oven.
4. Bake for about 20 minutes and take out.
5. Serve and enjoy!

**Serving Suggestions:** Serve with honey on the top.

**Variation Tip:** You can add herbs to enhance taste.

**Nutritional Information per Serving:**

**Calories:** 136 | **Fat:** 6.2g|**Sat Fat:** 2.1g|**Carbohydrates:** 6.2g|**Fiber:** 0g|**Sugar:** 6.2g|**Protein:** 13g

# Mushroom Spinach Egg Muffin

**Preparation Time:** 10 minutes
**Cooking Time:** 25 minutes
**Servings:** 2

**Ingredients:**

- ½ cup frozen spinach, chopped
- 1 cup mushrooms, chopped
- 4 eggs
- 2 tablespoons low-fat Greek yogurt
- Salt, to taste

**Preparation:**

1. Add eggs, yogurt, mushrooms, spinach, and salt in a large bowl. Beat well.
2. Preheat the baking oven to 375 degrees F and grease muffin tins.
3. Pour the mushroom batter in muffin tins and bake for about 25 minutes.
4. Take out, serve and enjoy!

**Serving Suggestions:** Serve with some sauce.

**Variation Tip:** Use cayenne pepper to enhance taste.

**Nutritional Information per Serving:**

**Calories:** 150 | **Fat:** 9.1g|**Sat Fat:** 2.8g|**Carbohydrates:** 5g|**Fiber:** 0.5g|**Sugar:** 4.2g|**Protein:** 13g

# Baked Eggs

**Preparation Time:** 10 minutes
**Cooking Time:** 9 minutes
**Servings:** 3

## Ingredients:

- 6 eggs
- 1 cup fresh spinach, chopped finely
- 6 tablespoons low-fat Parmesan cheese, shredded
- ¼ cup heavy cream
- Salt and black pepper, to taste

## Preparation:

1. Preheat the oven to 425 degrees F.
2. Grease 6 muffin tins and add spinach in them.
3. Add eggs on spinach and top them with heavy cream.
4. Add on parmesan cheese, salt and pepper.
5. Place muffin tins in baking oven and bake for about 9 minutes.
6. Take out and serve.

**Serving Suggestions:** Top with chopped spinach before serving.

**Variation Tip:** You can also use mozzarella cheese.

**Nutritional Information per Serving:**

**Calories:** 343 | **Fat:** 24.5g|**Sat Fat:** 13g|**Carbohydrates:** 3.3g|**Fiber:** 0.2g|**Sugar:** 0.7g|**Protein:** 29.6g

# Egg Avocado Toast

**Preparation Time:** 10 minutes
**Cooking Time:** 4 minutes
**Servings:** 2

## Ingredients:

- ½ avocado, peeled, pitted and chopped
- 2 boiled eggs, peeled and sliced
- ½ tablespoon fresh lemon juice
- 2 whole-wheat bread slices
- Salt and black pepper, to taste

## Preparation:

1. Add avocado, salt, lemon juice, and pepper in a bowl and mash properly.
2. Place bread slices on a non-stick pan and toast them for 2 minutes per side.
3. Spread avocado mixture on bread slices and top them with boiled egg slices.
4. Serve and enjoy!

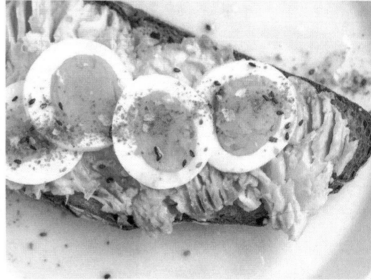

**Serving Suggestions:** Top with Roman coriander before serving.

**Variation Tip:** Replace black pepper with cayenne pepper.

## Nutritional Information per Serving:

**Calories:** 236 | **Fat:** 15.1g|**Sat Fat:** 3.7g|**Carbohydrates:** 16.3g|**Fiber:** 5.3g|**Sugar:** 2.2g|**Protein:** 10.2g

# Broccoli Waffles

**Preparation Time:** 10 minutes
**Cooking Time:** 8 minutes
**Servings:** 4

**Ingredients:**

- ½ cup chopped broccoli
- 2 eggs
- ½ cup low-fat cheddar cheese, shredded
- 1 teaspoon garlic powder
- 1 teaspoon dried onion, minced
- Salt and black pepper, to taste

**Preparation:**

1. Preheat and grease a waffle iron.
2. Meanwhile, add broccoli, cheddar cheese, eggs, dried onion, garlic powder, salt, and pepper in a large bowl. Mix well.
3. Pour the batter on the waffle-iron and cook for about 4 minutes.
4. Take out and serve.

**Serving Suggestions:** Serve with green chili sauce.

**Variation Tip:** You can omit ginger powder.

**Nutritional Information per Serving:**

**Calories:** 95 | **Fat:** 6.9g|**Sat Fat:** 3.7g|**Carbohydrates:** 1.7g|**Fiber:** 0.4g|**Sugar:** 0.6g|**Protein:** 6.7g

# Cheese Waffles

**Preparation Time:** 15 minutes
**Cooking Time:** 20 minutes
**Servings:** 8

## Ingredients:

- 2 eggs, beaten
- 2 garlic cloves, minced
- 2 cups ricotta cheese, crumbled
- 1 cup frozen spinach
- 1 cup part-skim mozzarella cheese, shredded
- ½ cup low-fat parmesan cheese, grated
- Salt and black pepper, to taste

## Preparation:

1. Grease and preheat a waffle iron.
2. Add eggs, garlic cloves, ricotta cheese and spinach in a large bowl. Beat well.
3. Now, add in mozzarella cheese, parmesan cheese, salt, and pepper. Whisk properly.
4. Pour the batter on the waffle-iron and cook for about 5 minutes.
5. Take out and serve hot.

**Serving Suggestions:** Serve with maple syrup on the top.

**Variation Tip:** You can omit spinach.

**Nutritional Information per Serving:**

**Calories:** 119 | **Fat:** 7g|**Sat Fat:** 4g|**Carbohydrates:** 3.9g|**Fiber:** 0.1g|**Sugar:** 0.3g|**Protein:** 10.2g

# Arugula Omelet

**Preparation Time:** 5 minutes
**Cooking Time:** 7 minutes
**Servings:** 2

**Ingredients:**

- 3 eggs
- 2 scallions, chopped finely
- 1 tablespoon unsweetened almond milk
- 1 tablespoon olive oil
- 1 cup fresh arugula, chopped finely
- Salt, to taste
- Black pepper, to taste

**Preparation:**

1. Add eggs, scallions, almond milk, arugula, salt, and pepper in a large bowl. Beat well.
2. Meanwhile, warm up olive oil in a non-stick pan.
3. Add egg mixture and cook it for about 5 minutes on low heat.
4. Take out the omelet and serve with bread.

**Serving Suggestions:** Serve with coriander leaves on the top.

**Variation Tip:** You can also add tomatoes in omelet.

**Nutritional Information per Serving:**

**Calories:** 163 | **Fat:** 13.8g|**Sat Fat:** 3.1g|**Carbohydrates:** 2.1g|**Fiber:** 0.6g|**Sugar:** 1.1g|**Protein:** 8.9g

# Eggs in Pepper Rings

**Preparation Time:** 15 minutes
**Cooking Time:** 6 minutes
**Servings:** 4

**Ingredients:**

- 2 bell peppers, seeded and cut into rings
- 8 eggs
- 2 tablespoons fresh chives, chopped
- 2 tablespoons fresh parsley, chopped
- Salt and pepper, to taste

**Preparation:**

1. Add bell pepper rings in a greased non-stick pan and cook for about 2 minutes.
2. Flip the rings and crack an egg in the middle of each ring.
3. Top with salt and pepper and cook for about 4 minutes.
4. Take out and top with parsley and chives.
5. Serve and enjoy!

**Serving Suggestions:** Top it with chopped coriander leaves.

**Variation Tip:** Use chili flakes on the top.

**Nutritional Information per Serving:**

**Calories:** 146 | **Fat:** 8.9g|**Sat Fat:** 2.7g|**Carbohydrates:** 5.4g|**Fiber:** 0.9g|
**Sugar:** 3.7g|**Protein:** 11.8g

# Basil Tomato Omelet

**Preparation Time:** 7 minutes
**Cooking Time:** 5 minutes
**Servings:** 4

**Ingredients:**

- 8 eggs
- 2 tablespoons olive oil
- ½ tablespoons red pepper flakes, crushed
- ½ cup basil, chopped
- 1 cup tomatoes, chopped
- Salt, to taste
- Black pepper, to taste

**Preparation:**

1. Add eggs, red pepper flakes, salt, and pepper in a large bowl. Beat well.
2. Add in tomatoes and basil. Whisk properly.
3. Meanwhile, add olive oil in a non-stick pan and add egg mixture in it.
4. Cook for about 5 minutes and take out.
5. Serve and enjoy!

**Serving Suggestions:** Top with cheese before serving.

**Variation Tip:** You can also add cayenne pepper to enhance taste.

**Nutritional Information per Serving:**

**Calories:** 197 | **Fat:** 16g|**Sat Fat:** 3.8g|**Carbohydrates:** 2.9g|**Fiber:** 0.8g|
**Sugar:** 1.9g|**Protein:** 11.6g

# Lunch Recipes

## Beef Lettuce Wraps

**Preparation Time:** 20 minutes
**Cooking Time:** 13 minutes
**Servings:** 4

**Ingredients:**

- 8 lettuce leaves
- 4 tablespoons white onion, chopped
- ¼ teaspoon onion powder
- 1¼ cups lean ground beef
- 4 tablespoons light thousand island dressing
- ¼ teaspoon white vinegar

**Preparation:**

1. Put a skillet over medium-high heat and sauté onions for about 3 minutes.
2. Add in beef and cook for about 10 minutes.
3. Take out and set aside for a while.
4. Meanwhile, add onion powder, dressing and vinegar in a large bowl. Mix well.
5. Add beef in the bowl and mix properly.
6. Arrange lettuce leaves on a plate and place beef mixture on them.
7. Serve and enjoy!

**Serving Suggestions:** Top with some sauce before serving.

**Variation Tip:** You can also use garlic powder for better taste.

**Nutritional Information per Serving:**

**Calories:** 155 | **Fat:** 7.7g|**Sat Fat:** 1.6g|**Carbohydrates:** 1.9g|**Fiber:** 0.3g|**Sugar:** 0.6g|**Protein:** 17.9g

# Salmon Lettuce Wraps

**Preparation Time:** 20 minutes
**Servings:** 4

**Ingredients:**

- 4 tablespoons fresh dill, chopped
- ½ cup low-fat mozzarella cheese, cubed
- 8 smoked salmon slices
- ½ cup chopped tomatoes
- 8 lettuce leaves
- 2 teaspoons fresh lemon juice
- Salt, to taste

**Preparation:**

1. Add smoked salmon, fresh dill, mozzarella cheese, chopped tomatoes, lemon juice, and salt in a large bowl. Mix properly.
2. Arrange lettuce leaves on plates and place salmon mixture on them.
3. Serve immediately.

**Serving Suggestions:** Top with some sauce before serving.

**Variation Tip:** You can also use soy sauce.

**Nutritional Information per Serving:**

**Calories:** 223 | **Fat:** 8.2g|**Sat Fat:** 2g|**Carbohydrates:** 3.1g|**Fiber:** 0.8g|**Sugar:** 0.7g|**Protein:** 33g

# Chicken Burger

**Preparation Time:** 25 minutes
**Cooking Time:** 10 minutes
**Servings:** 8

**Ingredients:**

- 3 pounds ground chicken
- 4 tablespoons olive oil
- 2 eggs
- 2 teaspoons dried thyme
- 1 yellow onion, grated
- 2 cucumbers, chopped
- 8 cups lettuce, torn
- Salt and black pepper, to taste

**Preparation:**

1. Add ground chicken, eggs, onion, olive oil, and dried thyme in a large bowl. Mix well.
2. Make patties out of the mixture and place them in a non-stick pan.
3. Cook patties for about 5 minutes per side and take out.
4. Meanwhile, place lettuce and cucumbers on buns and top them with patties.
5. Cover them with top side of the bun and serve.

**Serving Suggestions:** Top with chopped mint leaves before serving.

**Variation Tip:** You can use chili sauce to enhance taste.

**Nutritional Information per Serving:**

**Calories:** 424 | **Fat:** 20.9g|**Sat Fat:** 4.9g|**Carbohydrates:** 5.9g|**Fiber:** 1.1g|**Sugar:** 2.5g|**Protein:** 51.5g

# Turkey Meatballs

**Preparation Time:** 10 minutes
**Cooking Time:** 15 minutes
**Servings:** 2

**Ingredients:**

- ½ pound ground turkey
- 1 tablespoon olive oil
- ½ cup frozen chopped spinach, thawed and squeezed
- ¼ teaspoon dried oregano
- ¼ cup feta cheese, crumbled
- Salt and black pepper, to taste

**Preparation:**

1. Add ground turkey, spinach, oregano, cheese, salt, and pepper in a large bowl. Mix well.
2. Make 6 equal-sized balls out of the mixture and set aside.
3. Meanwhile, add oil in a non-stick skillet and place meatballs in it.
4. Cook for about 15 minutes and take out.
5. Serve and enjoy!

**Serving Suggestions:** Top with coriander leaves before serving.

**Variation Tip:** You can also add garlic powder to enhance taste.

**Nutritional Information per Serving:**

**Calories:** 333 | **Fat:** 23.5g|**Sat Fat:** 5.9g|**Carbohydrates:** 1.2g|**Fiber:** 0.3g| **Sugar:** 0.8g|**Protein:** 33.9g

# Italian Shrimp Meal

**Preparation Time:** 10 minutes
**Cooking Time:** 7 minutes
**Servings:** 2

**Ingredients:**

- 1 tablespoon olive oil
- ½ cup cherry tomatoes, quartered
- ½ garlic clove, minced
- 1 zucchini, chopped
- ¼ teaspoon red pepper flakes
- ¼ cup chicken broth
- ½ pound shrimp, peeled and deveined
- Salt and pepper, to taste

**Preparation:**

1. Warm up olive oil in a large non-stick skillet and sauté garlic and red pepper flakes for about 1 minute.
2. Add shrimp, salt and black pepper and cook for 1 minute per side.
3. Add in chicken broth and zucchini noodles and cook for about 4 minutes.
4. Stir in tomato quarters and take out.
5. Serve and enjoy!

**Serving Suggestions:** Top with coriander leaves before serving.

**Variation Tip:** You can also add soy sauce to enhance taste.

**Nutritional Information per Serving:**

**Calories:** 225 | **Fat:** 9.4g|**Sat Fat:** 1.7g|**Carbohydrates:** 7.3g|**Fiber:** 1.7g|
**Sugar:** 3g|**Protein:** 28.1g

# Asparagus Shrimp Meal

**Preparation Time:** 8 minutes
**Cooking Time:** 10 minutes
**Servings:** 2

### Ingredients:

- 3 tablespoons chicken broth
- 1 tablespoon olive oil
- 1 tablespoon fresh lemon juice
- ½ pound asparagus, trimmed
- 2 garlic cloves, minced
- ½ pound shrimp, peeled and deveined
- Salt and pepper, to taste

### Preparation:

1. Warm up oil in a large skillet over medium-high heat.
2. Add lemon juice, asparagus, garlic cloves, shrimp, salt and pepper in the skillet.
3. Cover the lid and cook for about 2 minutes.
4. Open the lid and cook for about 4 minutes, stir occasionally.
5. Add in broth and cook for 4 more minutes.
6. Take out and serve hot.

**Serving Suggestions:** Serve with tortilla.

**Variation Tip:** You can add vinegar to enhance taste.

### Nutritional Information per Serving:

**Calories:** 227 | **Fat:** 9.3g|**Sat Fat:** 1.7g|**Carbohydrates:** 7.4g|**Fiber:** 2.5g|**Sugar:** 2.4g|**Protein:** 29g

# Broccoli Scallops

**Preparation Time:** 20 minutes
**Cooking Time:** 9 minutes
**Servings:** 4

**Ingredients:**

- 4 tablespoons olive oil
- 2 teaspoons fresh lemon juice
- 2 cups broccoli, cut into small pieces
- 1-pound scallops
- 2 garlic cloves, crushed
- Salt and pepper, to taste

**Preparation:**

1. Warm up olive oil in a large skillet and add in broccoli and garlic.
2. Cook for about 4 minutes and stir occasionally.
3. Add in scallops and cook for about 4 minutes. Flip occasionally.
4. Add in lemon juice, salt and pepper. Stir well.
5. Take out and serve hot.

**Serving Suggestions:** You can serve with red chili sauce on the top.

**Variation Tip:** You can use both black pepper and cayenne pepper.

**Nutritional Information per Serving:**

**Calories:** 238 | **Fat:** 15g|**Sat Fat:** 2.1g|**Carbohydrates:** 6.3g|**Fiber:** 1.2g| **Sugar:** 0.8g|**Protein:** 20.4g

# Lemon Asparagus Scallops

**Preparation Time:** 20 minutes
**Cooking Time:** 10 minutes
**Servings:** 10

## Ingredients:

* 4 tablespoons olive oil
* 4 tablespoons fresh lemon juice
* ½ cup yellow onion, chopped
* 3 pounds baby scallops
* 4 garlic cloves, minced
* 4 teaspoons fresh lemon zest, grated
* 4 tablespoons fresh rosemary, minced
* 2 pounds fresh asparagus, chopped
* Salt and pepper, to taste

## Preparation:

1. Heat oil in a skillet and sauté onions for about 2 minutes.
2. Then, sauté garlic and rosemary for about 1 minute.
3. Now, add in lemon zest and asparagus in the skillet and cook for about 2 minutes.
4. Add in scallops and stir well.
5. Reduce the heat and cook for about 5 minutes. Stir occasionally.
6. Stir in salt, pepper, and lemon juice and take out.
7. Serve and enjoy!

**Serving Suggestions:** Top with roman coriander before serving.

**Variation Tip:** Rosemary can be omitted.

**Nutritional Information per Serving:**

**Calories:** 196 | **Fat:** 7g|**Sat Fat:** 1.1g|**Carbohydrates:** 8.8g|**Fiber:** 2.7g|**Sugar:** 2.1g|**Protein:** 25.1g

# Pan-Seared Scallops

**Preparation Time:** 12 minutes
**Cooking Time:** 11 minutes
**Servings:** 10

## Ingredients:

- 2 tablespoons olive oil
- 3½ cups fresh baby spinach
- 3 pounds jumbo sea scallops
- 12 garlic cloves, minced
- 2 cups onions, chopped
- Salt and black pepper, to taste

## Preparation:

1. Warm up olive oil in a large non-stick skillet and cook scallops with salt and pepper for about 2 minutes 30 seconds on each side in it.
2. Take the scallops out of the pan and set them aside.
3. Now, add onions and garlic in the same skillet and sauté for about 3 minutes.
4. Add in spinach and cook for about 3 minutes.
5. Take out and set spinach on serving plates.
6. Top with scallops and serve.

**Serving Suggestions:** Serve with tomato slices on the top.

**Variation Tip:** Use coconut oil instead of olive oil.

## Nutritional Information per Serving:

**Calories:** 170 | **Fat:** 4.2g|**Sat Fat:** 0.4g|**Carbohydrates:** 8.7g|**Fiber:** 1.6g|**Sugar:** 1.2g|**Protein:** 24.7g

# Vegetable Curry

**Preparation Time:** 20 minutes
**Cooking Time:** 25 minutes
**Servings:** 12

**Ingredients:**

- 2 tablespoons olive oil
- 6 cups fresh spinach
- 2 small yellow onions, chopped
- 2 pounds Brussels sprouts
- 2 teaspoons fresh thyme, chopped
- 2 cups fresh mushrooms, sliced
- Salt and black pepper, to taste

**Preparation:**

1. Heat oil in a non-stick skillet and sauté onions for about 4 minutes.
2. Now, sauté thyme and garlic for about 1 minute.
3. Add in mushrooms and cook for about 15 minutes.
4. Then, add in Brussels sprouts and stir properly.
5. Cook for about 3 minutes and stir in spinach.
6. Cook for about 4 minutes and stir in salt and pepper.
7. Take out and serve.

**Serving Suggestions:** Garnish with red chili flakes before serving.

**Variation Tip:** Use oregano to enhance taste.

**Nutritional Information per Serving:**

**Calories:** 64 | **Fat:** 2.7g|**Sat Fat:** 0.4g|**Carbohydrates:** 9g|**Fiber:** 3.6g|**Sugar:** 2.4g|**Protein:** 3.5g

# Dinner Recipes

## Taco Broccoli Bowl

**Preparation Time:** 7 minutes
**Cooking Time:** 12 minutes
**Servings:** 2

### Ingredients:

- ½ pound lean ground beef
- ¼ cup low-fat cheddar cheese
- 2 cups chopped broccoli
- ½ teaspoon garlic powder
- 4 tablespoons chicken broth
- ½ teaspoon onion powder
- ½ cup chopped tomatoes
- ¼ teaspoon red pepper flakes
- Salt, to taste

### Preparation:

1. Cook beef for about 10 minutes in a large skillet.
2. Meanwhile, add broccoli and broth in a microwave safe bowl and cover it with a plastic wrap.
3. Microwave for about 4 minutes and take out. Set aside.
4. In the skillet, add garlic powder, onion powder, salt, tomatoes, and red pepper flakes. Mix properly.
5. Now, add in broccoli and toss to coat well.
6. Take out and top with cheddar cheese.
7. Serve and enjoy!

**Serving Suggestions:** Top with onion rings before serving.

**Variation Tip:** You can also use mozzarella cheese.

### Nutritional Information per Serving:

**Calories:** 317 | **Fat:** 12.4g|**Sat Fat:** 5.7g|**Carbohydrates:** 9.2g|**Fiber:** 3.1g| **Sugar:** 3.3g|**Protein:** 41.7g

# Chicken Fajita Platter

**Preparation Time:** 7 minutes
**Cooking Time:** 25 minutes
**Servings:** 2

### Ingredients:

- ½ pound chicken breasts, cut into thin strips
- ½ teaspoon garlic powder
- ¼ green bell pepper, cut into strips
- ½ teaspoon ground cumin
- ¼ red bell pepper, cut into strips
- 1 teaspoon chili powder
- ½ onion, sliced
- ¼ teaspoon dried oregano
- 1 tablespoon olive oil
- Salt, to taste

### Preparation:

1. Preheat the oven to 400 degrees F.
2. Meanwhile, add chicken breast, garlic powder, green bell pepper, and red bell pepper in a bowl. Mix well.
3. Now, add in ground cumin, chili powder, onion, dried oregano, olive oil, and salt in the bowl. Mix properly.
4. Set the mixture on the baking dish and bake for about 25 minutes.
5. Take out and serve.

**Serving Suggestions:** Serve with green chili sauce on the top.

**Variation Tip:** Add vinegar to enhance taste.

**Nutritional Information per Serving:**

**Calories:** 313 | **Fat:** 15.8g|**Sat Fat:** 3.4g|**Carbohydrates:** 8.3g|**Fiber:** 2.4g| **Sugar:** 4.2g|**Protein:** 34.2g

# Lemon Chicken

**Preparation Time:** 8 minutes
**Cooking Time:** 17 minutes
**Servings:** 3

## Ingredients:

- 1 tablespoon olive oil
- 1 tablespoon fresh parsley, minced
- ½ pound skinless and boneless chicken breasts
- ½ teaspoon fresh lemon zest, grated finely
- 1 garlic clove, minced
- ½ pound yellow squash, sliced
- 1 tablespoon fresh lemon juice
- Salt and pepper, to taste

## Preparation:

1. Warm up olive oil in a skillet and fry chicken in it for about 8 minutes.
2. Take out and set aside.
3. Meanwhile, sauté garlic in the same skillet for about 1 minute and add in squash slices.
4. Cook for about 6 minutes and add chicken in it.
5. Stir well and cook for about 2 minutes.
6. Now, add lemon zest, lemon juice and parsley. Stir well and take out.
7. Serve and enjoy!

**Serving Suggestions:** Garnish with chopped coriander before serving.

**Variation Tip:** Almond oil can also be used.

## Nutritional Information per Serving:

**Calories:** 170 | **Fat:** 7.2g|**Sat Fat:** 1.4g|**Carbohydrates:** 3.1g|**Fiber:** 0.9g|**Sugar:** 1.5g|**Protein:** 23g

# Herbed Chicken

**Preparation Time:** 20 minutes
**Cooking Time:** 45 minutes
**Servings:** 12

**Ingredients:**

- ¾ pound skinless, boneless chicken thighs
- 2 teaspoons dried rosemary, crushed
- 6 broccoli heads, cut into florets
- 2 teaspoons dried oregano, crushed
- 8 garlic cloves, minced
- ½ cup extra-virgin olive oil
- Salt and pepper, to taste

**Preparation:**

1. Warm up the baking oven to 375 degrees F and grease a baking dish.
2. Meanwhile, add chicken thighs, dried rosemary, dried oregano, garlic cloves, salt, pepper, and oil. Toss to coat well.
3. Arrange broccoli florets in the bottom of a baking dish and top them with chicken thighs.
4. Bake for 45 minutes and take out.
5. Serve and enjoy!

**Serving Suggestions:** Serve with mint leaves on the top.

**Variation Tip:** Coconut oil can also be used.

**Nutritional Information per Serving:**

**Calories:** 127 | **Fat:** 9.6g|**Sat Fat:** 1.6g|**Carbohydrates:** 4g|**Fiber:** 1.4g|**Sugar:** 0.8g|**Protein:** 7.8g

# Asian Style Beef

**Preparation Time:** 10 minutes
**Cooking Time:** 16 minutes
**Servings:** 2

**Ingredients:**

- ½ pound sirloin steak
- 1 tablespoon fresh lime juice
- 1 tablespoon olive oil
- 1 tablespoon low-sodium soy sauce
- 1 garlic clove, minced
- 1 cup broccoli florets
- ½ Serrano pepper, seeded and chopped finely
- Salt and pepper, to taste

**Preparation:**

1. Marinade the steak slices with black pepper.
2. Meanwhile, warm up oil in a skillet and fry the steak slices for about 8 minutes.
3. Take out the slices and sauté garlic and Serrano pepper for about 1 minute.
4. Add in broccoli and stir for about 3 minutes.
5. Now, stir in steak slices, soy sauce and lemon juice.
6. Cook for about 4 minutes and take out.
7. Serve and enjoy!

**Serving Suggestions:** Top with dried parsley before serving.

**Variation Tip:** You can add dried cumin to enhance taste.

**Nutritional Information per Serving:**

**Calories:** 297 | **Fat:** 14.3g|**Sat Fat:** 3.7g|**Carbohydrates:** 6g|**Fiber:** 1.4g|**Sugar:** 1.7g|**Protein:** 36.4g

# Filling Beef Dish

**Preparation Time:** 5 minutes
**Cooking Time:** 10 minutes
**Servings:** 2

## Ingredients:

- 1 tablespoon olive oil
- 1½ tablespoons low-sodium soy sauce
- 2 garlic cloves, minced
- 1 cup fresh kale, chopped
- ½ pound beef sirloin steak, cut into bite-sized pieces
- 1 cup carrots, chopped
- Salt and pepper, to taste

## Preparation:

1. Warm up olive oil in a large skillet and sauté garlic for about 1 minute.
2. Add in beef and black pepper. Stir well.
3. Cook for about 4 minutes and add in kale, carrot and soy sauce.
4. Cook for about 5 minutes and stir in soy sauce and salt.
5. Take out and serve.

**Serving Suggestions:** Serve with tortilla.

**Variation Tip:** Add a pinch of cayenne pepper to enhance taste.

## Nutritional Information per Serving:

**Calories:** 328 | **Fat:** 14.1g|**Sat Fat:** 3.7g|**Carbohydrates:** 12.7g|**Fiber:** 1.9g| **Sugar:** 5.5g|**Protein:** 2.6g

# Spinach Haddock Fillets

**Preparation Time:** 15 minutes
**Cooking Time:** 17 minutes
**Servings:** 4

## Ingredients:

- 4 tablespoons olive oil
- 6 cups fresh baby spinach
- 8 garlic cloves, minced
- 4 (½ pound) haddock fillets
- 2 teaspoons fresh ginger, grated finely
- Salt and pepper, to taste

## Preparation:

1. Warm up 2 tablespoons oil in a large skillet and sauté 4 garlic cloves and ginger for about 1 minute.
2. Now, add haddock fillets, salt, and pepper and cook for about 5 minutes per side.
3. Meanwhile, warm up remaining oil in another skillet and sauté garlic for about 1 minute.
4. Add spinach, salt, and pepper and cook for about 5 minutes.
5. Set spinach on serving plates and place haddock fillets on them.
6. Serve and enjoy!

**Serving Suggestions:** Serve with chopped mint leaves on the top.

**Variation Tip:** You can also use white pepper.

## Nutritional Information per Serving:

**Calories:** 397 | **Fat:** 16.4g|**Sat Fat:** 2.4g|**Carbohydrates:** 4.3g|**Fiber:** 1.2g| **Sugar:** 0.3g|**Protein:** 56.7g

# Zucchini Halibut

**Preparation Time:** 10 minutes
**Cooking Time:** 20 minutes
**Servings:** 5

## Ingredients:

- 2 (½ pound) halibut steaks
- ½ teaspoon olive oil
- 2 tablespoons feta cheese, crumbled
- ¼ cup yellow onion, minced
- 1 cup fresh tomatoes, chopped
- ½ cup zucchini, chopped
- 1 tablespoon fresh basil, chopped
- 1 garlic clove, minced
- Salt and pepper, to taste

## Preparation:

1. Preheat the baking oven to 450 degrees F and oil a baking dish.
2. Meanwhile, heat oil in a skillet and sauté garlic, onion and zucchini in it for about 5 minutes.
3. Stir in tomatoes, basil and black pepper and remove the skillet from heat.
4. Now, place halibut steaks in the baking dish and top with zucchini mixture.
5. Sprinkle with cheese and bake for about 15 minutes.
6. Take out and serve hot.

**Serving Suggestions:** Serve with chili flakes on the top.

**Variation Tip:** You can also add black roman seeds.

**Nutritional Information per Serving:**

**Calories:** 3632 | **Fat:** 77.4g|**Sat Fat:** 10.9g|**Carbohydrates:** 2.7g|**Fiber:** 0.7g|
**Sugar:** 1.6g|**Protein:** 687.2g

# Seafood Feast

**Preparation Time:** 25 minutes
**Cooking Time:** 11 minutes
**Servings:** 10

## Ingredients:

- 6 tablespoons olive oil
- 1 teaspoon garlic, minced
- 2 pounds fresh asparagus, chopped
- 2 tablespoons dried parsley
- 4 red bell peppers, seeded and chopped
- ½ pound raw scallops
- ½ pound raw shrimp, peeled and deveined
- Salt and pepper, to taste

## Preparation:

1. Heat oil in a skillet and fry bell peppers and asparagus in it for about 5 minutes.
2. Take out and set aside.
3. Add shrimp and scallops in the skillet and fry for about 2 minutes.
4. Add in garlic, parsley, salt and pepper and cook for about 1 minute.
5. Stir in cooked vegetables and cook for about 3 minutes.
6. Take out and serve hot.

**Serving Suggestions:** Serve with mint leaves on the top.

**Variation Tip:** You can add lemon if you want.

## Nutritional Information per Serving:

**Calories:** 153 | **Fat:** 9.2g|**Sat Fat:** 1.4g|**Carbohydrates:** 8.2g|**Fiber:** 2.6g| **Sugar:** 4.1g|**Protein:** 11.5g

# Stuffed Chicken

**Preparation Time:** 7 minutes
**Cooking Time:** 25 minutes
**Servings:** 2

**Ingredients:**

- ½ tablespoon olive oil
- 2 (½ pound) boneless, skinless chicken breasts
- ½ small onion, chopped
- ¼ teaspoon dried oregano
- ½ pepperoni pepper, seeded and sliced thinly
- ½ cup fresh spinach, trimmed and chopped
- ¼ red bell pepper, seeded and sliced thinly
- ½ teaspoon minced garlic
- Salt and pepper, to taste

**Preparation:**

1. Warm up the baking oven to 350 degrees F and line a baking dish with a parchment paper.
2. Meanwhile, heat oil in a saucepan and sauté onion and peppers in it for about 1 minute.
3. Add in garlic and spinach and cook for about 3 minutes.
4. Stir in oregano, salt and pepper and remove the saucepan from heat.
5. Fill the chicken breasts with the spinach mixture and place them on a baking sheet.
6. Bake for about 20 minutes and take out.
7. Serve and enjoy!

**Serving Suggestions:** Serve with green chili sauce.

**Variation Tip:** You can omit dried oregano.

**Nutritional Information per Serving:**

**Calories:** 518 | **Fat:** 23.3g|**Sat Fat:** 6.3g|**Carbohydrates:** 5.7g|**Fiber:** 1.5g|**Sugar:** 1.5g|**Protein:** 69.1g

# Soups Recipes

## Chicken Soup

**Preparation Time:** 8 minutes
**Cooking Time:** 12 minutes
**Servings:** 2

**Ingredients:**

- 1 tablespoon olive oil
- 1 cup fresh kale, chopped
- ½ celery stalk, chopped
- ½ pound cooked chicken, shredded
- ½ carrot, peeled and chopped
- 2 cups chicken broth
- ½ yellow onion, chopped
- ¼ teaspoon dried thyme
- ¼ teaspoon dried oregano, crushed
- Salt and pepper, to taste

**Preparation:**

1. Warm up a pan and add oil in it.
2. Add in celery, onion, and carrot and cook for about 5 minutes.
3. Add pepper and herbs and cook for about 1 minute.
4. Stir in broth and cook for about 4 minutes.
5. Add chicken and kale. Stir well.
6. Cook for about 2 minutes and take out.
7. Serve and enjoy!

**Serving Suggestions:** Serve with crackers.

**Variation Tip:** Add vinegar to add some sour taste.

**Nutritional Information per Serving:**

**Calories:** 305 | **Fat:** 11.9g|**Sat Fat:** 2.4g|**Carbohydrates:** 8.8g|**Fiber:** 1.7g|**Sugar:** 2.7g|**Protein:** 39.2g

# Low-Carb Soup

**Preparation Time:** 8 minutes
**Cooking Time:** 23 minutes
**Servings:** 2

### Ingredients:

- ½ tablespoon olive oil
- ½ cup low-fat cheddar cheese, shredded
- ½ pound ground chicken
- 2 cups chicken broth
- ½ yellow onion, chopped
- ½ head cauliflower, chopped finely
- 1 garlic clove, minced
- Salt and black pepper, to taste

### Preparation:

1. Add oil in an Instant Pot and select "sauté".
2. Add in ground chicken and cook for about 4 minutes.
3. Add in onion and cook for about 3 minutes.
4. Add red pepper flakes and garlic and cook for about 1 minute.
5. Press "cancel" and add in broth, cauliflower, black pepper, and salt. Stir well.
6. Close the lid of Instant Pot and cook for about 15 minutes on "high pressure".
7. Press "cancel" and open the lid.
8. Add in cheddar and stir until melted.
9. Serve and enjoy!

**Serving Suggestions:** Serve with dried oregano on the top.

**Variation Tip:** Olive oil can be replaced with mustard oil.

**Nutritional Information per Serving:**

**Calories:** 428 | **Fat:** 22.7g|**Sat Fat:** 9.2g|**Carbohydrates:** 7.9g|**Fiber:** 2.3g| **Sugar:** 3.6g|**Protein:** 46.4g

# Turkey Soup

**Preparation Time:** 8 minutes
**Cooking Time:** 25 minutes
**Servings:** 2

## Ingredients:

- 1½ cups chicken broth
- 1 tablespoon olive oil
- 1 cup zucchini, chopped
- ½ yellow onion, chopped
- 1 cup cooked turkey meat, chopped
- ½ tablespoon garlic, minced
- 1 teaspoon fresh rosemary, chopped
- Salt and black pepper, to taste

## Preparation:

1. Add oil in an Instant Pot and select Sauté button.
2. Add in onion and cook for about 5 minutes.
3. Then place garlic and rosemary and cook for about 5 minutes.
4. Press the "cancel" button and add in turkey, zucchini, and chicken broth. Stir well.
5. Close the lid of Instant Pot and cook for about 5 minutes.
6. Open the lid and cook for about 8 minutes.
7. Take out and serve.

**Serving Suggestions:** Top with coriander before serving.

**Variation Tip:** Use cayenne pepper for an even better taste.

## Nutritional Information per Serving:

**Calories:** 310 | **Fat:** 14.5g|**Sat Fat:** 3.3g|**Carbohydrates:** 8.1g|**Fiber:** 1.5g|**Sugar:** 4.1g|**Protein:** 35g

# Turkey Cabbage Soup

**Preparation Time:** 7 minutes
**Cooking Time:** 30 minutes
**Servings:** 2

**Ingredients:**

- ½ tablespoon mustard oil
- ½ teaspoon ground ginger
- ½ pound lean ground turkey
- 2 tablespoons low-sodium soy sauce
- ½ onion, chopped
- 1½ cups chicken broth
- ½ cup carrot, peeled and shredded
- ¼ head cabbage, chopped
- Salt and black pepper, to taste

**Preparation:**

1. Add oil and turkey in an Instant Pot and press "sauté".
2. Cook the turkey for about 5 minutes and add in ginger, soy sauce, and onion. Stir well.
3. Now, add in chicken broth, carrot, cabbage, salt and pepper. Stir properly.
4. Close the lid of Instant Pot and cook for about 25 minutes.
5. Press "cancel" and open the lid.
6. Take out and serve hot.

**Serving Suggestions:** Squeeze lemon juice on the top.

**Variation Tip:** You can also use olive oil.

**Nutritional Information per Serving:**

**Calories:** 350 | **Fat:** 15.5g|**Sat Fat:** 4g|**Carbohydrates:** 14.3g|**Fiber:** 3.6g|**Sugar:** 8.3g|**Protein:** 38.3g

# Sirloin Steak Soup

**Preparation Time:** 20 minutes
**Cooking Time:** 36 minutes
**Servings:** 8

## Ingredients:

- 4 tablespoons olive oil
- 4 teaspoons garlic powder
- 2 pounds sirloin steak, trimmed and cubed
- 2 bay leaves
- 2 carrots, peeled and chopped
- 3 tablespoons fresh oregano, chopped
- 2 bell peppers, seeded and chopped
- 2 cups crushed tomatoes
- 2 celery stalks, chopped
- 3 cups water
- 2 onions, chopped
- 4 cups beef broth
- 2 cups fresh mushrooms, sliced
- Salt and pepper, to taste

## Preparation:

1. Warm up oil in a large pan and cook steak for about 5 minutes.
2. Add carrots, celery, bell peppers, and onions and cook for about 3 minutes.
3. Then, add mushrooms and cook for about 5 minutes. Stir occasionally.
4. Close the lid for about 3 minutes and add all the remaining ingredients.
5. Cook for about 15 minutes and take out.
6. Serve and enjoy!

**Serving Suggestions:** Before serving, garnish with mint leaves.

**Variation Tip:** You can also use chili sauce to enhance taste.

## Nutritional Information per Serving:

**Calories:** 356 | **Fat:** 15.1g|**Sat Fat:** 3.9g|**Carbohydrates:** 14.7g|**Fiber:** 4.5g|**Sugar:** 8g|**Protein:** 40.1g

# Beef Soup

**Preparation Time:** 10 minutes
**Cooking Time:** 23 minutes
**Servings:** 2

**Ingredients:**

- 1 tablespoon olive oil
- ¼ onion, sliced
- 1½ cups bok choy, chopped
- 1 garlic clove, minced
- 1½ cups water
- ½ teaspoon fresh ginger, minced
- 1 tablespoon low-sodium soy sauce
- ½ pound beef tenderloin, trimmed and cut into chunks
- 1 tablespoon balsamic vinegar
- Salt and black pepper, to taste

**Preparation:**

1. Add oil in an Instant Pot and select "sauté".
2. Add ginger, garlic and onion and cook for about 3 minutes.
3. Press "cancel" and add in water, soy sauce, beef tenderloin, balsamic vinegar, salt, and pepper. Stir well.
4. Close the lid of Instant Pot and cook for about 20 minutes.
5. Release the pressure and open the lid.
6. Add in bok choy and cook for about 10 minutes.
7. Take out and serve hot.

**Serving Suggestions:** Garnish with cilantro before serving.

**Variation Tip:** You can also use mint leaves for an even better taste.

**Nutritional Information per Serving:**

**Calories:** 332 | **Fat:** 17.8g|**Sat Fat:** 5g|**Carbohydrates:** 6.9g|**Fiber:** 2.3g|
**Sugar:** 3.4g|**Protein:** 36.5g

# Beef Spinach Soup

**Preparation Time:** 25 minutes
**Cooking Time:** 30 minutes
**Servings:** 8

## Ingredients:

- 2 tablespoons olive oil
- 2 pounds ground beef
- 8 cups fresh spinach, chopped
- 2 teaspoons ground ginger
- 2 onions, chopped
- 2 cups carrots, peeled and chopped
- 8 cups chicken broth
- Salt and pepper, to taste

## Preparation:

1. Add oil and beef in an Instant Pot and select "sauté".
2. Cook for about 5 minutes and press "cancel".
3. Add broth, spinach, ginger, onions, carrots, salt and pepper in the Instant Pot. Stir well.
4. Close the lid of Instant Pot and cook for about 25 minutes on High Pressure.
5. Press "cancel" and release the pressure.
6. Open the lid and take out the soup.
7. Serve and enjoy!

**Serving Suggestions:** Garnish cilantro on the top before serving.

**Variation Tip:** You can also use beef broth.

## Nutritional Information per Serving:

**Calories:** 310 | **Fat:** 12.1g|**Sat Fat:** 3.6g|**Carbohydrates:** 7.6g|**Fiber:** 2g|**Sugar:** 3.4g|**Protein:** 40.7g

# Green Beans Soup

**Preparation Time:** 10 minutes
**Cooking Time:** 38 minutes
**Servings:** 6

### Ingredients:

- 2 tablespoons olive oil
- 8 cups beef broth
- 2 onions, chopped
- 1-pound green beans, chopped
- 2 tablespoons garlic, minced
- 4 cups fresh tomatoes, chopped
- 4 teaspoons dried thyme, crushed
- 2 teaspoons ground cumin
- Salt and black pepper, to taste

### Preparation:

1. Add onion, garlic, cumin, and thyme in an Instant Pot and press "sauté" button.
2. Cook for about 3 minutes and press "cancel" button.
3. Stir in beans, broth and tomatoes and close the lid.
4. Cook for about 30 minutes on low pressure and release the pressure.
5. Open the lid, add in salt and pepper and stir well.
6. Take out and serve immediately.

**Serving Suggestions:** Top with chili sauce before serving.

**Variation Tip:** Use soy sauce to enhance taste.

**Nutritional Information per Serving:**

**Calories:** 160 | **Fat:** 7.1g|**Sat Fat:** 1.3g|**Carbohydrates:** 16.4g|**Fiber:** 5.2g| **Sugar:** 6.8g|**Protein:** 9.7g

# Salmon Soup

**Preparation Time:** 5 minutes
**Cooking Time:** 4 hours
**Servings:** 2

### Ingredients:

- ½ pound salmon fillets
- 2 tablespoons fresh parsley, chopped
- 2 tablespoons olive oil
- 1½ cups chicken broth
- ½ cup carrots, peeled and chopped
- ½ cup cauliflower, chopped
- ¼ cup celery stalk, chopped
- 2 tablespoons chopped yellow onion
- Salt and black pepper, to taste

### Preparation:

1. Add salmon fillets, parsley, olive oil, broth, carrots, cauliflower, celery stalk, onion, salt and pepper in a slow cooker.
2. Stir well and close the lid.
3. Cook for about 4 hours and open the lid.
4. Take out and serve.

**Serving Suggestions:** Serve with crackers.

**Variation Tip:** You can also add vinegar and soy sauce.

### Nutritional Information per Serving:

**Calories:** 401 | **Fat:** 24.9g|**Sat Fat:** 4.1g|**Carbohydrates:** 8.1g|**Fiber:** 1.9g| **Sugar:** 4.5g|**Protein:** 36.4g

# Tofu Soup

**Preparation Time:** 8 minutes
**Cooking Time:** 7 minutes
**Servings:** 2

## Ingredients:

- ½ tablespoon olive oil
- 1 cup medium broccoli florets
- 1 cup extra-firm tofu, pressed, drained and cubed
- ¼ teaspoon ground turmeric
- ¾ cup vegetable broth
- 1½ teaspoons red curry powder
- ¾ cup carrot, peeled and chopped
- 1 teaspoon ground ginger
- Salt and black pepper, to taste

## Preparation:

1. Add oil in an Instant Pot and select "sauté".
2. Add in tofu and sear for about 3 minutes.
3. Select "cancel" and add in broccoli, turmeric, vegetable broth, red curry powder, carrot, ginger, salt and pepper. Stir well.
4. Close the lid of Instant Pot and cook for about 4 minutes on High pressure.
5. Release the pressure and open the lid.
6. Take out and serve immediately.

**Serving Suggestions:** Squeeze lemon before serving.

**Variation Tip:** Turmeric can be omitted.

**Nutritional Information per Serving:**

**Calories:** 117 | **Fat:** 6.9g|**Sat Fat:** 0.9g|**Carbohydrates:** 10.8g|**Fiber:** 1.4g|**Sugar:** 2.6g|**Protein:** 7.8g

# Salads Recipes

## Berry Salad

**Preparation Time:** 20 minutes
**Servings:** 8

**Ingredients:**

- 4 tablespoons extra-virgin olive oil
- 2 cups fresh strawberries, hulled and sliced
- 10 cups fresh arugula
- 1 cup fresh blackberries
- 1 cup fresh raspberries
- 1 cup fresh blueberries
- Salt and black pepper, to taste

**Preparation:**

1. Add olive oil, strawberries, arugula, blackberries, raspberries, blueberries, pepper, and salt in a large bowl.
2. Toss to coat well, serve and enjoy!

**Serving Suggestions:** Top it with mint leaves.

**Variation Tip:** Almond oil can also be used.

**Nutritional Information per Serving:**

**Calories:** 104 | **Fat:** 7.5g|**Sat Fat:** 1g|**Carbohydrates:** 9.9g|**Fiber:** 3.5g|**Sugar:** 5.6g|**Protein:** 1.5g

# Citrus Fruit Salad

**Preparation Time:** 5 minutes
**Servings:** 2

**Ingredients:**

- 1 orange, peeled and segmented
- ½ cup fresh strawberries, hulled and sliced
- 2 cups fresh baby arugula
- 1 teaspoon extra-virgin olive oil
- 1 tablespoon fresh lemon juice
- Salt and pepper, to taste

**Preparation:**

1. Add orange, strawberries, arugula, oil, salt, and pepper in a large bowl.
2. Toss to coat well and squeeze lemon on the top.
3. Serve and enjoy!

**Serving Suggestions:** Top with mint leaves before serving.

**Variation Tip:** You can also add stevia.

**Nutritional Information per Serving:**

**Calories:** 82 | **Fat:** 2.7g|**Sat Fat:** 0.4g|**Carbohydrates:** 14.5g|**Fiber:** 3.3g|**Sugar:** 10.9g|**Protein:** 1.7g

# Cucumber Salad

**Preparation Time:** 10 minutes
**Servings:** 4

**Ingredients:**

- 1½ cucumbers, sliced thinly
- 3 cups lettuce, torn
- 1 cup tomatoes, chopped
- ½ tablespoon fresh lemon juice
- 2 tablespoons olive oil
- 1 tablespoon balsamic vinegar
- Salt and black pepper, to taste

**Preparation:**

1. Add cucumbers, tomatoes and lettuce in a bowl. Mix properly.
2. Then, add in lemon juice, olive oil, vinegar, salt, and pepper. Toss to coat well.
3. Serve and enjoy!

**Serving Suggestions:** Serve with fresh cucumber juice.

**Variation Tip:** You can also add dried oregano.

**Nutritional Information per Serving:**

**Calories:** 137 | **Fat:** 7.7g|**Sat Fat:** 1.2g|**Carbohydrates:** 18.1g|**Fiber:** 2.9g| **Sugar:** 8.6g|**Protein:** 3.3g

# Avocado Chicken Salad

**Preparation Time:** 20 minutes
**Servings:** 4

## Ingredients:

- 2 cups cooked chicken, shredded
- 2 teaspoons Dijon mustard
- 2 avocados, chopped
- ½ cup low-fat plain Greek yogurt
- 2 tablespoons fresh lime juice
- ¼ teaspoon cayenne pepper
- Salt, to taste

## Preparation:

1. Add avocados and lime juice in a large bowl. Mash well.
2. Now, add yogurt, cayenne pepper, salt, and Dijon mustard. Mix properly.
3. In the end, add in shredded chicken and mix well.
4. Serve and enjoy!

**Serving Suggestions:** Top with mint leaves before serving.

**Variation Tip:** You can add some spices too.

## Nutritional Information per Serving:

**Calories:** 336 | **Fat:** 21.9g|**Sat Fat:** 4.7g|**Carbohydrates:** 11.9g|**Fiber:** 6.9g|**Sugar:** 2g|**Protein:** 25.4g

# High-Protein Salad

**Preparation Time:** 10 minutes
**Servings:** 2

**Ingredients:**

- 2 boneless, skinless chicken breasts, shredded
- 1½ lettuce, torn
- 1 tablespoon olive oil
- 1½ fresh baby greens
- ¼ cup cherry tomatoes, halved
- Salt and black pepper, to taste

**Preparation:**

1. Add each ingredient in a large bowl and toss to coat well.
2. Serve and enjoy!

**Serving Suggestions:** Top with onion rings before serving.

**Variation Tip:** You can also add cilantro to enhance taste.

**Nutritional Information per Serving:**

**Calories:** 447 | **Fat:** 17.7g|**Sat Fat:** 3.9g|**Carbohydrates:** 24.7g|**Fiber:** 9.5g|**Sugar:** 2.1g|**Protein:** 49.6g

# Apple Strawberry Salad

**Preparation Time:** 10 minutes
**Servings:** 2

## Ingredients:

- ½ apple, chopped
- ½ cup fresh strawberries
- 1 cup cooked chicken, cubed
- 2 cups lettuce, torn
- 1 tablespoon apple cider vinegar
- 1 tablespoon extra-virgin olive oil
- Salt and black pepper, to taste

## Preparation:

1. Add apple, strawberries, lettuce and chicken in a large bowl. Mix well.
2. Now, add apple cider vinegar, extra-virgin olive oil, salt and pepper in the bowl and toss to coat well.
3. Serve and enjoy!

**Serving Suggestions:** Garnish with whipped cream before serving.

**Variation Tip:** You can add a little bit of allspice to enhance taste.

## Nutritional Information per Serving:

**Calories:** 215 | **Fat:** 9.4g|**Sat Fat:** 1.6g|**Carbohydrates:** 12.2g|**Fiber:** 2.4g| **Sugar:** 8.1g|**Protein:** 20.9g

# Spinach Tomato Salad

**Preparation Time:** 10 minutes
**Servings:** 4

**Ingredients:**

- 1½ cups cucumber, sliced
- 4 cups fresh spinach, torn
- 1½ cups cherry tomatoes, halved
- 2 tablespoons fresh mint leaves
- ½ cup onion, sliced

**Preparation:**

1. Add cucumber, spinach, cherry tomatoes, and onion in a large bowl. Mix well.
2. Top with mint leaves and serve.

**Serving Suggestions:** Top with cheese before serving.

**Variation Tip:** You can some lemon in the salad.

**Nutritional Information per Serving:**

**Calories:** 80 | **Fat:** 0.8g|**Sat Fat:** 0.2g|**Carbohydrates:** 17.5g|**Fiber:** 4.9g| **Sugar:** 9.6g|**Protein:** 4.2g

# Salmon Salad

**Preparation Time:** 25 minutes
**Servings:** 4

**Ingredients:**

- 1½ cups wild cooked salmon, chopped
- 4 tablespoons fresh lemon juice
- 2 cups cucumber, sliced
- 4 tablespoons olive oil
- 2 cups red bell pepper, sliced
- 2 cups fresh spinach, torn
- 1 cup grape tomatoes, quartered
- 2 cups lettuce, torn
- 2 tablespoons scallion, chopped
- Salt and black pepper, to taste

**Preparation:**

1. Add salmon, spinach, lettuce, cucumber, red bell pepper, tomatoes, and scallion in a large bowl. Mix well.
2. Now, add lemon juice, olive oil, salt and pepper in the bowl. Toss to coat well.
3. Serve and enjoy!

**Serving Suggestions:** You can serve with mint juice.

**Variation Tip:** You can use oregano to enhance taste.

**Nutritional Information per Serving:**

**Calories:** 491 | **Fat:** 29.7g|**Sat Fat:** 4.3g|**Carbohydrates:** 10.1g|**Fiber:** 2.3g| **Sugar:** 5.8g|**Protein:** 49.6g

# Shrimp Salad

**Preparation Time:** 7 minutes
**Cooking Time:** 3 minutes
**Servings:** 2

## Ingredients:

- ½ pound shrimp, peeled and deveined
- 2 tablespoons fresh cilantro
- 2 tablespoons green olives
- 1 tablespoon olive oil
- 2 tablespoons chopped onion
- 1 teaspoon fresh lemon juice
- 1 tomato, sliced
- Salt and black pepper, to taste

## Preparation:

1. Add oil in a pan and fry shrimp for about 3 minutes.
2. Take out and add shrimp in a large bowl.
3. Then, add cilantro, olives, onion, lemon juice, tomato, salt and pepper in the bowl and toss to coat well.
4. Serve and enjoy!

**Serving Suggestions:** Top with chopped basil leaves before serving.

**Variation Tip:** You can also use BBQ sauce to enhance taste.

## Nutritional Information per Serving:

**Calories:** 217| **Fat:** 10.1g|**Sat Fat:** 1.8g|**Carbohydrates:** 4.8g|**Fiber:** 1g| **Sugar:** 1.3g|**Protein:** 26.4g

# Scallop Salad

**Preparation Time:** 7 minutes
**Cooking Time:** 6 minutes
**Servings:** 2

**Ingredients:**

- ¾ pound fresh sea scallops, side muscles removed
- ½ garlic clove, minced
- 3 tablespoons olive oil
- 3 cups mixed baby greens
- 1 tablespoon fresh lemon juice
- 2 tablespoons yellow grape tomatoes, halved
- 2 tablespoons red grape tomatoes, halved
- Salt and black pepper, to taste

**Preparation:**

1. In a pan, heat 2 tablespoons olive oil and fry scallops in it for about 3 minutes per side.
2. Meanwhile, add garlic clove, remaining olive oil, baby greens, lemon juice, red tomatoes, yellow tomatoes, salt and pepper in a large bowl. Mix well.
3. Top with fried scallops and serve immediately.

**Serving Suggestions:** Top with chopped vinegar before serving.

**Variation Tip:** Use mustard oil instead of olive oil.

**Nutritional Information per Serving:**

**Calories:** 432 | **Fat:** 22.9g|**Sat Fat:** 3.2g|**Carbohydrates:** 24.4g|**Fiber:** 6.2g|
**Sugar:** 2.2g|**Protein:** 35g

# Part II Fueling Hacks Recipes

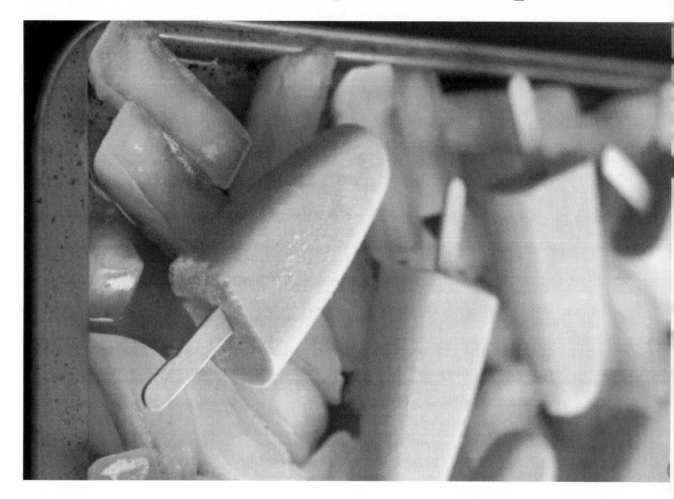

# Berry Mojito

**Preparation Time:** 10 minutes
**Servings:** 1

**Ingredients:**

- ½ cup water
- 1 teaspoon Mixed Berry Flavor Infuser
- 3 fresh mint leaves
- 1 tablespoon fresh lime juice
- Ice cubes, as required

**Preparation:**

1. Take a cocktail glass and divide the lime juice and mint leaves in the bottom.
2. With the bottom end of a spoon, gently muddle the mint leaves.
3. Now, add the Berry Infuser and water into the glass and stir to combine.
4. Add ice cubes to the glass.
5. Serve and enjoy!

**Serving Suggestions:** Garnish it with lemon wedges and mint leaves.

**Variation Tip:** You can use frozen berries if you do not have fresh ones.

**Nutritional Information per Serving:**

**Calories:** 26 | **Fat:** 0.3g|**Sat Fat:** 0.1g|**Carbohydrates:** 6.6g|**Fiber:** 2.5g|
**Sugar:** 0.7g|**Protein:** 1.3g

# Vanilla Shake

**Preparation Time:** 5 minutes
**Servings:** 1

**Ingredients:**

- ½ cup water
- 1 teaspoon Vanilla Shake Fueling
- ½ cup unsweetened almond milk
- 1 teaspoon Gingerbread Fueling
- 8 ice cubes

**Preparation:**

1. Take a blender, place all ingredients, and pulse until smooth.
2. Pour in serving glasses and serve.

**Serving Suggestions:** Garnish it with whipped cream and sprinkle chocolate over it.

**Variation Tip:** You can also use ice cream to prepare a thick milkshake.

**Nutritional Information per Serving:**

**Calories:** 130 | **Fat:** 3.3g|**Sat Fat:** 0.2g|**Carbohydrates:** 15g|**Fiber:** 4.5g|
**Sugar:** 6g|**Protein:** 13g

# Mint Cookies

**Preparation Time:** 15 minutes
**Cooking Time:** 10 minutes
**Servings:** 2

**Ingredients:**

- 1 egg white
- 1 tablespoon unsweetened almond milk
- 2 teaspoons Essential Mint Chocolate Cookie Bars
- 2 teaspoons Essential Decadent Double Chocolate Brownie

**Preparation:**

1. Preheat the oven to 350 degrees F. Line a cooking utensil with parchment paper.
2. In a food processor, add the Chocolate Bars and pulse until fully crushed.
3. Transfer crushed bar into a bowl with other ingredients and mix until well blended.
4. Using a spoon place 4 cookies onto the prepared cookie sheet in a single layer and press each ball slightly with your fingers.
5. Bake for about 13-15 minutes.
6. Remove it from the oven and let it cool for about 5 minutes onto a wire rack.
7. Now, invert the cookies onto the wire rack to cool before serving.

**Serving Suggestions:** Garnish with powdered sugar.

**Variation Tip:** Adding brown sugar can make your cookies softer.

**Nutritional Information per Serving:**

**Calories:** 175 | **Fat:** 6.1g|**Sat Fat:** 2.5g|**Carbohydrates:** 20.7g|**Fiber:** 1.3g| **Sugar:** 14.1g|**Protein:** 9.8g

# Mocha Cake

**Preparation Time:** 5 minutes
**Cooking Time:** 2 minutes
**Servings:** 2

## Ingredients:

- ¼ cup water
- ¼ teaspoon baking powder
- 1 tablespoon egg beaters
- 2 teaspoons Splenda
- 2 teaspoons Chocolate Chip Pancakes
- 2 teaspoons Calorie Burn Cappuccino

## Preparation:

1. Take a bowl, add all ingredients and stir till good mingling.
2. Place the mixture into the microwave for 1-2 minutes.
3. Take it out from the microwave and divide it into two parts.
4. Serve warm.

**Serving Suggestions:** Top with extra crunch and some cacao nibs.

**Variation Tip:** You can also use sugar instead of Splenda.

## Nutritional Information per Serving:

**Calories:** 195 | **Fat:** 4.5g|**Sat Fat:** 1g|**Carbohydrates:** 28.9g|**Fiber:** 2.5g|**Sugar:** 11g|**Protein:** 11g

# Pumpkin Waffles

**Preparation Time:** 10 minutes
**Cooking Time:** 8 minutes
**Servings:** 4

**Ingredients:**

- ½ cup water
- 4 tablespoons sugar-free pancake syrup
- Pinch of ground cinnamon
- ½ teaspoon pumpkin pie spice
- 2 tablespoons 100% canned pumpkin
- 4 teaspoons Golden Pancake

**Preparation:**

1. Heat a mini waffle iron so grease it.
2. In a bowl, add all ingredients apart from flapjack sweetener and blend till well integrated.
3. Place half the mixture into the preheated waffle iron and cook for 3-4 minutes or till golden brown.
4. Repeat with the remaining mixture.
5. Serve warm and enjoy!

**Serving Suggestions:** Serve with butter, syrup, and pumpkin seeds.

**Variation Tip:** You can also use honey instead of syrup.

**Nutritional Information per Serving:**

**Calories:** 148 | **Fat:** 3.1g|**Sat Fat:** 0.3g|**Carbohydrates:** 27.5g|**Fiber:** 3.2g| **Sugar:** 11.4g|**Protein:** 3.6g

# Chocolate Donuts

**Preparation Time:** 15 minutes
**Cooking Time:** 27½ minutes
**Servings:** 4

## Ingredients:

- ½ teaspoon vanilla extract
- ½ teaspoon baking powder
- ¼ cup unsweetened almond milk
- 6 tablespoons liquid egg substitute
- 4 teaspoons Essential Chocolate Chip Pancakes
- 4 teaspoons Double Brownie

## Preparation:

1. Preheat the oven to 350 degrees F. Lightly grease 4 holes of a donut pan.
2. Take a bowl, add all ingredients, and mix until well blended.
3. Place the mixture into the prepared donut pan evenly.
4. Bake for about 12-15 minutes or until donuts is set completely.
5. Remove from the oven and set aside to cool slightly.
6. Serve warm.

**Serving Suggestions:** Serve with chocolate chip or crushed Oreos on top.

**Variation Tip:** You can use any kind of milk.

## Nutritional Information per Serving:

**Calories:** 212 | **Fat:** 7.2g|**Sat Fat:** 1.5g|**Carbohydrates:** 31.1g|**Fiber:** 1.6g| **Sugar:** 11.2g|**Protein:** 6.4g

# Chicken Nuggets

**Preparation Time:** 10 minutes
**Cooking Time:** 20 minutes
**Servings:** 4

**Ingredients:**

- 2 tablespoons olive oil
- 1 egg
- 4 teaspoons Essential Honey Mustard & Onion Sticks (finely crushed)
- ¾ pound boneless, skinless chicken breast (cubed)
- 3 tablespoons lemon juice

**Preparation:**

1. Preheat the oven to 400 degrees F. Line a baking sheet with a lightly greased piece of foil.
2. Take a bowl, crack the egg, and beat well.
3. Take another bowl, place the crushed Onion Sticks.
4. Dip the chicken cubes in beaten egg and then coat with crushed sticks.
5. Arrange the coated chicken cubes onto the prepared baking sheet in a single layer and spray with cooking spray.
6. Bake for about 18-20 minutes, flipping once halfway through.
7. Remove the baking sheet from the oven and set the nuggets aside to cool slightly.
8. Serve warm!

**Serving Suggestions:** Serve with ketchup or any other sauce of your taste.

**Variation Tip:** You can add any kind of seasoning mix according to your taste.

**Nutritional Information per Serving:**

**Calories:** 134 | **Fat:** 3.4g|**Sat Fat:** 0.4g|**Carbohydrates:** 4.6g|**Fiber:** 0.8g|**Sugar:** 2.3g|**Protein:** 19.9g

# Vanilla Frappe

**Preparation Time:** 5 minutes
**Servings:** 1

**Ingredients:**

- ½ cup ice
- 1 tablespoon whipped topping
- 1 cup unsweetened almond milk
- 2 tablespoons Essential Vanilla Shake

**Preparation:**

1. Take a blender and add the given amount of Vanilla Shake, almond milk and ice.
2. Blend them well until smooth.
3. Pour the mixture into a glass.
4. Top it with whipped cream.
5. Serve and enjoy!

**Serving Suggestions:** you can add cherry or some berries for presentation.

**Variation Tip:** Use coconut syrup for extraordinary taste.

**Nutritional Information per Serving:**

**Calories:** 308 | **Fat:** 11.2g|**Sat Fat:** 1.5g|**Carbohydrates:** 10.4g|**Fiber:** 9g| **Sugar:** 2.2g|**Protein:** 41.1g

# Chocolate Popsicles

**Preparation Time:** 5 minutes
**Servings:** 6

**Ingredients:**

- 1 teaspoon vanilla extract
- 4 teaspoons zero-calorie sugar substitute
- 6 teaspoons Dark Chocolate Cherry Shake
- 2 cups plain low-fat Greek yogurt
- 1 tablespoon instant espresso powder
- 1 cup unsweetened almond milk

**Preparation:**

1. Pour almond milk in a mug and microwave on High for about 45 seconds.
2. Remove the mug from the microwave and immediately stir in the espresso powder until dissolved completely.
3. Set aside to cool completely.
4. In a blender, add the cooled espresso milk and remaining ingredients and pulse until smooth.
5. Divide the mixture into 6 large Popsicle molds and freeze overnight before serving.

**Serving Suggestions:** Sprinkle chocolate chips on top.

**Variation Tip:** Coconut milk can also be used.

**Nutritional Information per Serving:**

**Calories:** 51 | **Fat:** 1.7g|**Sat Fat:** 0.8g|**Carbohydrates:** 4.2g|**Fiber:** 0.3g| **Sugar:** 3.4g|**Protein:** 4.4g

# Tropical Smoothie Bowl

**Preparation Time:** 10 minutes
**Servings:** 2

**Ingredients:**

- 2 tablespoons unsweetened coconut, shredded
- 1 teaspoon chia seeds
- 1 teaspoon lime zest, grated
- 2 tablespoons cashews
- 1 cup ice cubes
- 1 cup unsweetened coconut milk
- 4 teaspoons Essential Tropical Fruit Smoothie

**Preparation:**

1. In a blender, add the Smoothie bag, coconut milk, and ice cubes and pulse until sleek.
2. Take a serving bowl and add the mixture to it.
3. Top with remaining ingredients.
4. Take a serving bowl and add the mixture to it.
5. Top with remaining ingredients.
6. Serve and enjoy!

**Serving Suggestions:** Top with a variety of toppings such as berries, coconut, or seeds.

**Variation Tip:** You can also add chocolate syrup to enhance the taste.

**Nutritional Information per Serving:**

**Calories:** 944 | **Fat:** 41.2g|**Sat Fat:** 28.6g|**Carbohydrates:** 142.1g|**Fiber:** 12.5g|**Sugar:** 103.1g|**Protein:** 8.5g

# Chia Seed Pudding

**Preparation Time:** 10 minutes
**Cooking Time:** 11 minutes
**Servings:** 1

**Ingredients:**

- 1 cup unsweetened almond milk
- ¼ cup chia seeds
- 4 teaspoons Chia Bliss Smoothie

**Preparation:**

1. In a serving bowl, add all the ingredients and mix until well blended.
2. Refrigerate overnight before serving.

**Serving Suggestions:** Mix it with honey and vanilla for extra sweetness.

**Variation Tip:** You can also use coconut milk.

**Nutritional Information per Serving:**

Calories: 414 | **Fat:** 13.7g|**Sat Fat:** 1.5g|**Carbohydrates:** 67g|**Fiber:** 15.4g| **Sugar:** 48g|**Protein:** 8.2g

# Brownie Pudding Cups

**Preparation Time:** 10 minutes
**Cooking Time:** 1 minutes
**Servings:** 2

## Ingredients:

- 2 teaspoons Chocolate Pudding Mix
- 2 tablespoons sugar-free caramel syrup
- 1 cup water, divided
- 2 teaspoons Brownie Mix

## Preparation:

1. In a bowl, add the Pudding Mix and 3 tablespoons of water and mix well.
2. Divide the mixture equally and microwave for a minute.
3. Take it out from the microwave and chill it down completely.
4. In a bowl, add the Pudding combine and remaining water, and mix well.
5. Place the pudding mixture over the brownie mixture equally.
6. Drizzle the very best with caramel sweetening and with a knife swirl caramel into pudding.
7. Refrigerate until set completely before serving.

**Serving Suggestions:** Top with chocolate syrup before serving.

**Variation Tip:** you can also use caramel syrup for a taste.

**Nutritional Information per Serving:**

**Calories:** 106 | **Fat:** 2.1g|**Sat Fat:** 0.4g|**Carbohydrates:** 21.8g|**Fiber:** 0.5g| **Sugar:** 0g|**Protein:** 0.6g

# Potato Bagel

**Preparation Time:** 15 minutes
**Cooking Time:** 12 minutes
**Servings:** 2

**Ingredients:**

- 4 egg whites
- 2 teaspoons baking powder
- 4 teaspoons Mashed Potatoes

**Preparation:**

1. Preheat the oven to 350 degrees F.
2. Spread oil lightly in the holes of a donut pan.
3. Take a bowl, add the egg whites and beat until foamy.
4. Add baking powder and mashed potatoes and beat until well blended.
5. Place the mixture into the prepared donut hole.
6. Bake for about 10-12 minutes. Check if it is completely baked.
7. Serve warm.

**Serving Suggestions:** Serve warm with some butter.

**Variation Tip:** You can also use sweet potatoes.

**Nutritional Information per Serving:**

**Calories:** 106 | **Fat:** 1.1g|**Sat Fat:** 0.4g|**Carbohydrates:** 15.7g|**Fiber:** 0.1g|**Sugar:** 0.5g|**Protein:** 9.1g

# Maple Pancakes

**Preparation Time:** 10 minutes
**Cooking Time:** 6 minutes
**Servings:** 1

**Ingredients:**

- ¼ cup water
- 1 tablespoon sugar-free pancake syrup
- ¼ teaspoon ground cinnamon
- 2 teaspoons stevia
- 1 tablespoon egg beaters
- ¼ teaspoon baking powder
- 1 Maple Brown Sugar Oatmeal

**Preparation:**

1. Add all the given ingredients in an exceeding bowl.
2. Combine them until well mixed.
3. Gently grease the pan and warm it on medium-high. Place the mixture in the oven.
4. Cook till its golden brown.
5. Serve and enjoy when it's still warm.

**Serving Suggestions:** Serve with the topping of pomegranate seeds.

**Variation Tip:** You can also add maple syrup to enhance the taste.

**Nutritional Information per Serving:**

**Calories:** 11 | **Fat:** 2.5g|**Sat Fat:** 0.5g|**Carbohydrates:** 33.2g|**Fiber:** 3.3g|**Sugar:** 9.1g|**Protein:** 5.9g

# Peanut Butter Cookies

**Preparation Time:** 10 minutes
**Cooking Time:** 12 minutes
**Servings:** 4

**Ingredients:**

- ¼ teaspoon vanilla extract
- 1/8 teaspoon sea salt
- 1 tablespoon margarine, softened
- ¼ cup unsweetened almond milk
- ¼ teaspoon baking powder
- 8 teaspoons Silky Peanut Butter Shake

**Preparation:**

1. Heat the oven to 350 degrees F.
2. Take a bowl and add the paste Shake and leaven and blend well.
3. Add the almond milk, oleomargarine, and flavoring and blend till well intermingled.
4. Place cookies onto the ready cookware in an exceedingly single layer.
5. Using a fork, press every ball slightly.
6. Sprinkle each cookie with salt.
7. Take it out from the home appliance and place the cooking utensil onto a wire rack to cool down for relating to 5 minutes.
8. Serve and enjoy.

**Serving Suggestions:** Serve with chocolate chip toppings.

**Variation Tip:** You can also use natural peanut butter.

**Nutritional Information per Serving:**

**Calories:** 589 | **Fat:** 34.6g|**Sat Fat:** 11.5g|**Carbohydrates:** 64.4g|**Fiber:** 0.1g| **Sugar:** 53.5g|**Protein:** 9.1g

# Tiramisu Shake

**Preparation Time:** 5 minutes
**Servings:** 2

**Ingredients:**

- 1 cup water
- 1 cup ice, crushed
- 2 tablespoons sugar-free chocolate syrup
- 4 teaspoons Cappuccino mix

**Preparation:**

1. In a small blender, add all the ingredients and pulse until smooth and creamy.
2. Pour the shake into a serving glass.
3. Serve and enjoy!

**Serving Suggestions:** You can serve with chocolate syrup and whipped cream on top.

**Variation Tip:** You can also decorate with additional ladyfinger cookies.

**Nutritional Information per Serving:**

**Calories:** 106 | **Fat:** 3g|**Sat Fat:** 1g|**Carbohydrates:** 17g|**Fiber:** 0g|**Sugar:** 10g|**Protein:** 1g

# Little Fudge Balls

**Preparation Time:** 10 minutes
**Servings:** 2

**Ingredients:**

- 4 tablespoons peanut butter powder
- ¼ cup unsweetened almond milk
- 2 tablespoons water
- 2 teaspoons Chocolate shake
- 2 teaspoons Chocolate pudding

**Preparation:**

1. In an exceedingly little bowl, add all the ingredients and blend till well combined.
2. Make eight little equal-sized balls from the mixture.
3. Organize the balls onto a parchment paper-lined baking sheet and refrigerate till set before serving.

**Serving Suggestions:** Serve with chocolate sprinkles on top.

**Variation Tip:** You can also use coconut milk.

**Nutritional Information per Serving:**

**Calories:** 538 | **Fat:** 14.3g|**Sat Fat:** 7.2g|**Carbohydrates:** 81.8g|**Fiber:** 5.8g| **Sugar:** 57.5g|**Protein:** 24.5g

# Brownie Cookies

**Preparation Time:** 10 minutes
**Cooking Time:** 2 minutes 20 seconds
**Servings:** 2

## Ingredients:

- 3 tablespoons water
- 2 teaspoons Brownie mix
- 1 peanut Butter Chocolate Crunch Bar

## Preparation:

1. In a bowl, add the brownie mix and water and mix well. Set aside.
2. In a microwave-safe bowl, place the crunch bar and microwave on High for about 20 seconds or until it is slightly melted.
3. Add the crunch bar into the brownie mixture and mix until well combined.
4. Divide the mixture into 2 greased ramekins and microwave on High for about 2 minutes.
5. Remove from microwave and set aside to cool for about 5 minutes before serving.
6. Enjoy!

**Serving Suggestions:** Top with your favorite type of nuts or use chocolate chips.

**Variation Tip:** You can also use milk chocolate or white chocolate chunks.

## Nutritional Information per Serving:

**Calories:** 186 | **Fat:** 6.1g|**Sat Fat:** 2.1g|**Carbohydrates:** 25.8g|**Fiber:** 2g| **Sugar:** 6g|**Protein:** 8.6g

# Mini Chocolate Cakes

**Preparation Time:** 10 minutes
**Cooking Time:** 18 minutes
**Servings:** 2

## Ingredients:

- ¼ cup water
- ¼ teaspoon baking powder
- 2 teaspoons Brownie Mix
- 2 teaspoons Chocolate Chip Pancakes

## Preparation:

1. Heat the kitchen appliance to 350 degrees F.
2. Add all the ingredients in an exceeding bowl, blend them well.
3. Place the mixture into the greased bread cups equally.
4. Bake for fifteen minutes.
5. Take it out from the oven let them sit for some time.
6. Refrigerate the muffins for a better taste.
7. Serve and enjoy!

**Serving Suggestions:** Serve with chocolate syrup and sprinkles on top.

**Variation Tip:** you can also use gluten-free flour or cake flour if needed.

## Nutritional Information per Serving:

**Calories:** 197 | **Fat:** 6.6g|**Sat Fat:** 1.4g|**Carbohydrates:** 32.1g|**Fiber:** 0.5g|
**Sugar:** 6g|**Protein:** 3.6g

# Flavorsome Waffles

**Preparation Time:** 18 minutes
**Cooking Time:** 8 minutes
**Servings:** 2

## Ingredients:

- ¼ cup water
- 2 teaspoons sugar-free pancake syrup
- 1 tablespoon 100% canned pumpkin
- ¼ teaspoon pumpkin pie spice
- 2 teaspoons Chocolate Chip Pancakes

## Preparation:

1. Heat a mini waffle iron so grease it.
2. In a bowl, add all the ingredients aside from hot cake sweetener and blend till well combined.
3. Place ½ of the mixture into preheated waffle iron and cook for concerning 3-4 minutes or till golden brown.
4. Repeat with the remaining mixture.
5. Serve warm!

**Serving Suggestions:** Serve with the topping of pancake syrup.

**Variation Tip:** Add strawberries on top for even better taste.

## Nutritional Information per Serving:

**Calories:** 139 | **Fat:** 4.6g|**Sat Fat:** 1g|**Carbohydrates:** 21.8g|**Fiber:** 0.8g| **Sugar:** 6.3g|**Protein:** 3.1g

# Richly Tasty Crepe

**Preparation Time:** 10 minutes
**Cooking Time:** 4 minutes
**Servings:** 1

## Ingredients:

- 1/8 teaspoon vanilla extract
- 1 teaspoon sugar-free chocolate syrup
- 1 teaspoon stevia powder
- ¼ cup part-skim ricotta cheese
- ¼ cup water
- 2 teaspoons Chocolate Chip Pancakes

## Preparation:

1. In a bowl, add the pancake and water and blend well.
2. Heat a gently lubricated frypan over medium heat.
3. Place the mixture and unfold during a skinny circle.
4. Cook for 1-2 minutes per facet or till golden brown.
5. Take it out and place the crepe onto a plate.
6.  In a little bowl, add the cheese, stevia, and vanilla extract and blend till well combined.
7. Place the mixture within the crepe.
8. Serve and enjoy!

**Serving Suggestions:** Drizzle with chocolate syrup on top.

**Variation Tip:** Add hazelnuts to enhance the taste.

## Nutritional Information per Serving:

**Calories:** 365 | **Fat:** 13.9g|**Sat Fat:** 5.1g|**Carbohydrates:** 47.3g|**Fiber:** 1.1g|**Sugar:** 13.9g|**Protein:** 13.1g

# Crunchy Cookies

**Preparation Time:** 10 minutes
**Cooking Time:** 15 minutes
**Servings:** 2

**Ingredients:**

- 2 teaspoons stevia powder
- ½ teaspoon vanilla extract
- 1/8 teaspoon baking powder
- 1/3 cup water
- 1/8 teaspoon ground cinnamon
- 2 teaspoons Oatmeal
- 2 teaspoons Oatmeal Raisin Crunch Bar

**Preparation:**

1. Heat the kitchen appliance to 350 degrees F. Line a kitchen utensil with parchment paper.
2. In associate passing microwave-safe bowl, place the crunch bar and microwave on High for regarding fifteen seconds or until it's slightly liquefied.
3. At intervals in the bowl of the bar, add the remaining ingredients and mix until well combined.
4. Set the mixture aside for regarding 5 minutes.
5. With a spoon, place four cookies onto the prepared cookware in associate passing single layer, and at the side of your fingers, press each ball slightly.
6. Bake for regarding 12-15 minutes or until golden brown.
7. Remove from the kitchen appliance and place the cookware onto a wire rack to chill down for regarding 5 minutes.
8. Now, invert the cookies onto the wire rack to chill down before serving.

**Serving Suggestions:** Serve with chocolate chips on top.

**Variation Tip:** You can use brown sugar for taste.

**Nutritional Information per Serving:**

**Calories:** 110 | **Fat:** 2.1g|**Sat Fat:** 0.9g|**Carbohydrates:** 16g|**Fiber:** 3.4g|**Sugar:** 2.8g|**Protein:** 7.3g

# Delish French toast Sticks

**Preparation Time:** 15 minutes
**Cooking Time:** 4 minutes
**Servings:** 3

## Ingredients:

- 2 tablespoons low-fat cream cheese, softened
- Olive Oil Cooking spray
- 6 tablespoons egg liquid substitute
- 4 teaspoons Essential Cinnamon Crunchy Oat Cereal

## Preparation:

1. In a food processor, add the cereal sachets and pulse till fine breadcrumbs like consistency are achieved.
2. Add the egg liquid substitute and cheese and pulse till a dough form.
3. Divide the dough into half a dozen parts and form every into a breadstuff.
4. Heat a gently lubricated pan over medium-high heat and cook the dish sticks for concerning a pair of minutes per facet or till golden brown.
5. Serve warm.

**Serving Suggestions:** Top with icing sugar before serving.

**Variation Tip:** You can add honey to enhance the taste.

**Nutritional Information per Serving:**

**Calories:** 120 | **Fat:** 3g|**Sat Fat:** 1.5g|**Carbohydrates:** 17.7g|**Fiber:** 1.3g|
**Sugar:** 5.6g|**Protein:** 6.4g

# Shamrock Shake

**Preparation Time:** 5 minutes
**Servings:** 1

**Ingredients:**

- ¼ teaspoon peppermint extract
- 2 drops green food coloring
- 1 cup ice cubes
- 12 cups unsweetened almond milk
- 2 teaspoons Vanilla Shake

**Preparation:**

1. In a blender, place all ingredients and pulse till swish.
2. Transfer the shake into a serving glass and serve forthwith.

**Serving Suggestions:** Top it with whipping cream.

**Variation Tip:** Add an extra hint of vanilla to the shake for best taste.

**Nutritional Information per Serving:**

**Calories:** 250 | **Fat:** 10.9g|**Sat Fat:** 1.2g|**Carbohydrates:** 30.5g|**Fiber:** 3.7g| **Sugar:** 7.1g|**Protein:** 10.7g

# Peppermint Mocha

**Preparation Time:** 5 minutes
**Servings:** 1

## Ingredients:

- ¼ teaspoon Velvety Hot Chocolate peppermint extract
- 1 tablespoon whipped topping
- Pinch of ground cinnamon
- ¼ cup warm unsweetened almond milk
- 12 cups freshly brewed coffee
- 2 teaspoons Essential Velvety Hot Chocolate

## Preparation:

1. In a serving mug, place the Hot Chocolate sachet, coffee, almond milk, and peppermint extract and stir until well blended.
2. Top the hot chocolate with whipped topping and sprinkle with cinnamon.
3. Serve immediately.

**Serving Suggestions:** Garnish with crushed candy cranes.

**Variation Tip:** You can use any coffee available at the moment.

## Nutritional Information per Serving:

**Calories:** 61 | **Fat:** 3.7g | **Sat Fat:** 1.9g | **Carbohydrates:** 5.4g | **Fiber:** 0.6g | **Sugar:** 4g | **Protein:** 1.1g

# Pumpkin Frappe

**Preparation Time:** 5 minutes
**Servings:** 1

## Ingredients:

- ½ cup ice
- 1 tablespoon whipped topping
- 1/8 teaspoon pumpkin pie spice
- 8 teaspoons unsweetened almond milk
- 8 teaspoons strong brewed coffee
- 2 teaspoons Essential Spiced Gingerbread

## Preparation:

1. In a blender, add the Spiced Gingerbread sachet, coffee, almond milk, pumpkin pie spice, and ice and pulse until smooth.
2. Transfer the mixture into a glass and top with whipped topping.
3. Serve immediately.
4. Enjoy!

**Serving Suggestions:** Serve with your favorite sprinkles on top.

**Variation Tip:** Pour in an extra shot of espresso according to taste.

## Nutritional Information per Serving:

**Calories:** 28 | **Fat:** 7.3g|**Sat Fat:** 0.6g|**Carbohydrates:** 21.4g|**Fiber:** 1.5g| **Sugar:** 9.3g|**Protein:** 1.7g

# No-Bake Chocolate Haystacks

**Preparation Time:** 10 minutes

**Servings:** 2

**Ingredients:**

- 2 teaspoons stevia powder
- 2 teaspoons Cinnamon Pretzel Sticks, crushed
- 1 tablespoon peanut butter powder
- 3 tablespoons water
- 2 teaspoons Brownie Mix

**Preparation:**

1. In a small bowl, add the brownie mix and water and mix until paste forms.
2. Add peanut butter powder and stevia and mix until well combined.
3. Add the crushed pretzels and mix until well combined.
4. With a spoon, place 6 haystacks onto a piece of foil and freeze for about 1 hour or until set.
5. Serve and Enjoy!

**Serving Suggestions:** Garnish with your favorite sprinkles.

**Variation Tip:** Mini marshmallows and other nuts are another possible add-ins.

**Nutritional Information per Serving:**

**Calories:** 137 | **Fat:** 3g|**Sat Fat:** 3.6g|**Carbohydrates:** 15.5g|**Fiber:** 5.1g|
**Sugar:** 4.5g|**Protein:** 15g

# Eggnog

**Preparation Time:** 10 minutes
**Servings:** 1

## Ingredients:

- 1 organic egg (yolk and white separated)
- ¼ tsp. rum extract
- Pinch of ground nutmeg
- 2 teaspoons Essential Vanilla Shake
- 16 cups unsweetened almond milk

## Preparation:

1. In a blender, add the Vanilla Shake bag, almond milk, and ingredient and pulse till sleek.
2. Within the bowl of a stand mixer, place albumen and beat on medium speed till stiff peaks type.
3. Place the whipped egg whites into a serving glass and top with shake mixture.
4. Stir the mixture and sprinkle with nutmeg.
5. Serve straight off.

**Serving Suggestions:** Serve with whipped cream on the top.

**Variation Tip:** You can also add chocolate or maple syrup for a taste.

## Nutritional Information per Serving:

**Calories:** 349 | **Fat:** 18.5g|**Sat Fat:** 8.3g|**Carbohydrates:** 34.8g|**Fiber:** 2.5g|**Sugar:** 23.1g|**Protein:** 12.1g

# Marshmallow Cereal Treat

**Preparation Time:** 5 minutes
**Cooking Time:** 1 minute
**Servings:** 1

## Ingredients:

- 2 tablespoons marshmallow dip
- 2 teaspoons Berry Cereal Crunch

## Preparation:

1. In a tiny bowl, add the Cereal Crunch and candy dip and blend well.
2. Place the mixture into a microwave-safe mini loaf pan and with the rear of a spoon, press slightly.
3. Microwave for concerning one minute.
4. Take away from the microwave and put aside to chill utterly before serving.

**Serving Suggestions:** Serve with extra marshmallows on top.

**Variation Tip:** Do not over stir the mixture after adding the cereal.

**Nutritional Information per Serving:**

**Calories:** 170 | **Fat:** 4g|**Sat Fat:** 2g|**Carbohydrates:** 32g|**Fiber:** 0g|**Sugar:** 14g|**Protein:** 2g

# Sandwich Cookies

**Preparation Time:** 15 minutes
**Cooking Time:** 12 minutes
**Servings:** 1

## Ingredients:

- 1 tablespoon whipped cream
- 3 tablespoons water
- 1/8 teaspoon baking powder
- 2 teaspoons Chocolate Chip Soft Bake

## Preparation:

1. Heat the kitchen appliance to 375 degrees F. Line a utensil with parchment paper.
2. In a bowl, mix on the Chocolate Bake bag and leaven.
3. Slowly, add the water and mix until well mingling.
4. Divide the dough in 2 things and place onto the prepared cookware.
5. Together with your hands, press each dough piece
6. Bake for twelve minutes.
7. Cast off from the home appliance and place the cookware onto a wire rack to relax for relating to 5 minutes.
8. Now, invert the cookies onto the wire rack to relax before serving.
9. Organize cookie, sleek aspect upwards.
10. Place the primping on top of the cookie.
11. Cowl with the remaining cookie and gently press on.
12. Serve and enjoy!

**Serving Suggestions:** Add crushed Oreos on top.

**Variation Tip:** Add Malted milk for a bit of butterscotch note.

## Nutritional Information per Serving:

**Calories:** 44 | **Fat:** 8.6g|**Sat Fat:** 3.9g|**Carbohydrates:** 15.7g|**Fiber:** 1g|**Sugar:** 8g|**Protein:** 2.3g

# 5 & 1 Plan

## Week 1

### DAY 1

**Fueling Hacks:**

Berry Mojito

Vanilla Shake

Mint Cookies

Mocha Cake

Pumpkin Waffles

**Lean & Green Meal:**

Cheddar Broccoli Bread

### DAY 2

**Fueling Hacks:**

Chocolate Donuts

Chicken Nuggets

Pizza Bites

Chocolate Popsicles

Tropical Smoothie bowl

**Lean & Green Meal:**

Lemon Asparagus Scallops

### DAY 3

**Fueling Hacks:**

Chia Seed Pudding

Brownie Pudding Cups

Potato Bagel

Maple Pancakes

Peanut Butter Cookies

**Lean & Green Meal:**

Herbed Chicken

### DAY 4

**Fueling Hacks:**

Tiramisu Shake

Little Fudge Balls

Brownie Cookies

Mini Chocolate Cakes

Flavorsome Waffles

**Lean & Green Meal:**

Turkey Soup

### DAY 5

**Fueling Hacks:**

Richly Tasty Crepe

Crunchy Cookies

Delish French Toast Sticks

Shamrock Shake

Peppermint Mocha

**Lean & Green Meal:**

Sian-Style Beef

### DAY 6

**Fueling Hacks:**

Pumpkin Frappe

No Bake Chocolate Haystacks

Eggnog

Marshmallow Cereal Treat

Sandwich Cookies

**Lean & Green Meal:**

Zucchini Halibut

### DAY 7

**Fueling Hacks:**

Berry Mojito

Vanilla Shake

Mint Cookies

Mocha Cake

Pumpkin Waffles

**Lean & Green Meal:**

Avocado Chicken Salad

# Week 2

## DAY 1

**Fueling Hacks:**

Chocolate Donuts

Chicken Nuggets

Pizza Bites

Chocolate Popsicles

Tropical Smoothie bowl

**Lean & Green Meal:**

Tofu Soup

## DAY 2

**Fueling Hacks:**

Chia Seed Pudding

Brownie Pudding Cups

Potato Bagel

Maple Pancakes

Peanut Butter Cookies

**Lean & Green Meal:**

Salmon Lettuce Wraps

## DAY 3

**Fueling Hacks:**

Tiramisu Shake

Little Fudge Balls

Brownie Cookies

Mini Chocolate Cakes

Flavorsome Waffles

**Lean & Green Meal:**

Herbed Chicken

## DAY 4

**Fueling Hacks:**

Richly Tasty Crepe

Crunchy Cookies

Delish French Toast Sticks

Shamrock Shake

Peppermint Mocha

**Lean & Green Meal:**

Sirloin Steak Soup

## DAY 5

**Fueling Hacks:**

Pumpkin Frappe

No Bake Chocolate Haystacks

Eggnog

Marshmallow Cereal Treat

Sandwich Cookies

**Lean & Green Meal:**

Chicken Fajita Platter

## DAY 6

**Fueling Hacks:**

Berry Mojito

Vanilla Shake

Mint Cookies

Mocha Cake

Pumpkin Waffles

**Lean & Green Meal:**

Vegetable Curry

## DAY 7

**Fueling Hacks:**

Chocolate Donuts

Chicken Nuggets

Pizza Bites

Chocolate Popsicles

Tropical Smoothie bowl

**Lean & Green Meal:**

Seafood Feast

# Week 3

## DAY 1

**Fueling Hacks:**

Vanilla Shake

Mint Cookies

Marshmallow Cereal Treat

No Bake Chocolate Haystacks

Chia Seed Pudding

**Lean & Green Meal:**

Salmon Lettuce Wraps

## DAY 2

**Fueling Hacks:**

Shamrock Shake

Chocolate Popsicles

Potato Bagel

Brownie Cookies

Richly Tasty Crepes

**Lean & Green Meal:**

Stuffed Chicken

## DAY 3

**Fueling Hacks:**

Tiramisu Shake

No Bake Chocolate Haystacks

Marshmallow Cereal Treat

Sandwich Cookies

Potato Bagel

**Lean & Green Meal:**

Avocado Chicken Salad

## DAY 4

**Fueling Hacks:**

Eggnog

Brownie Pudding Cups

Maple Pancakes

Flavorsome Waffles

Mini Chocolate Cakes

**Lean & Green Meal:**

Beef Spinach Soup

## DAY 5

**Fueling Hacks:**

Shamrock Shake

Chocolate Donuts

Sandwich Cookies

Maple Pancakes

Potato Bagel

**Lean & Green Meal:**

Asian Style Beef

## DAY 6

**Fueling Hacks:**

Mint Cookies

Chocolate Popsicles

Chia Seed Pudding

Potato Bagel

Peanut Butter Cookies

**Lean & Green Meal:**

Zucchini Halibut

## DAY 7

**Fueling Hacks:**

Eggnog

Marshmallow Cereal Treat

Brownie Pudding Cups

Maple Pancakes

Brownie Cookies

**Lean & Green Meal:**

Chicken Fajita Platter

# Week 4

## DAY 1

**Fueling Hacks:**

Berry Mojito

Mint Cookies

Chia Seed Pudding

Potato Bagel

Peanut Butter Cookies

**Lean & Green Meal**

Taco Broccoli Bowl

## DAY 2

**Fueling Hacks:**

Shamrock Shake

Chocolate Popsicles

Brownie Pudding Cups

Potato Bagel

Chia Seed Pudding

**Lean & Green Meal:**

Lemon Chicken

## DAY 3

**Fueling Hacks:**

Vanilla Shake

Tropical Smoothie Bowl

Chocolate Popsicles

Sandwich Cookies

Chicken Nuggets

**Lean & Green Meal:**

Low-Carb Soup

## DAY 4

**Fueling Hacks:**

Vanilla Frappe

Maple Pancakes

Brownie Cookies

No-Bake Chocolate Haystacks

Delish French Toast Sticks

**Lean & Green Meal:**

Asian Style Beef

## DAY 5

**Fueling Hacks:**

Eggnog

Marshmallow Cereal Treat

No-Bake Chocolate Haystacks

Brownie Pudding Cups

Peanut Butter Cookies

**Lean & Green Meal:**

## DAY 6

**Fueling Hacks:**

Tiramisu Shake

Chocolate Popsicles

Potato Bagel

Maple Pancakes

Tropical Smoothie Bowl

**Lean & Green Meal:**

Turkey Cabbage Soup

## DAY 7

**Fueling Hacks:**

Vanilla Shake

Chocolate Donuts

Mint Cookies

Chia Seed Pudding

Brownie Pudding Cups

**Lean & Green Meal:**

Taco Broccoli Bowl

# 4 & 2 & 1 Plan

## Week 1

### DAY 1

**Fueling Hacks:**

Berry Mojito

Vanilla Shake

Mint Cookies

Tropical Smoothie Bowl

**Lean & Green Meal:**

Chicken Soup

Asparagus Shrimp Meal

**Snack:**

½ cup canned peaches (packed in water or natural juices)

### DAY 2

**Fueling Hacks:**

Chocolate Donuts

Chicken Nuggets

Pizza Bites

Chocolate Popsicles

**Lean & Green Meal:**

Asian Style Beef

Turkey Meatballs

**Snack:**

¾ cup low-fat plain yogurt

### DAY 3

**Fueling Hacks:**

Chia Seed Pudding

Brownie Pudding Cups

Potato Bagel

Maple Pancakes

**Lean & Green Meal:**

Pan-Seared Scallops

Vegetable Curry

**Snack:**

4 ounces apple

### DAY 4

**Fueling Hacks:**

Tiramisu Shake

Little Fudge Balls

Brownie Cookies

Mini Chocolate Cakes

**Lean & Green Meal:**

Taco Broccoli Bowl

Chicken Fajita Platter

**Snack:**

3 celery stalks

### DAY 5

**Fueling Hacks:**

Richly Tasty Crepe

Crunchy Cookies

Delish French Toast Sticks

Shamrock Shake

**Lean & Green Meal:**

Lemon Chicken

Green Beans Soup

**Snack:**

½ ounce almonds

### DAY 6

**Fueling Hacks:**

Pumpkin Frappe

No Bake Chocolate Haystacks

Eggnog

Marshmallow Cereal Treat

**Lean & Green Meal:**

Asian Style Beef

Filling Beef Dish

**Snack:**

4 ounces orange

**DAY 7**

**Fueling Hacks:**

Berry Mojito

Vanilla Shake

Mint Cookies

Mocha Cake

**Lean & Green Meal:**

Spinach Haddock Fillets

Zucchini Halibut

**Snack:**

1 cup unsweetened cashew milk

# Week 2

**DAY 1**

**Fueling Hacks:**

Chocolate Donuts

Chicken Nuggets

Pizza Bites

Chocolate Popsicles

**Lean & Green Meal:**

Seafood Feast

Stuffed Chicken

**Snack:**

2 Dill Pickle Spears

**DAY 2**

**Fueling Hacks:**

Chia Seed Pudding

Brownie Pudding Cups

Potato Bagel

Maple Pancakes

**Lean & Green Meal:**

Cheddar Broccoli Bread

Beef Soup

**Snack:**

½ cup fresh strawberries

**DAY 3**

**Fueling Hacks:**

Tiramisu Shake

Little Fudge Balls

Brownie Cookies

Mini Chocolate Cakes

**Lean & Green Meal:**

Spinach Haddock Fillets

Chicken Burgers

**Snack:**

½ ounce cashews

**DAY 4**

**Fueling Hacks:**

Richly Tasty Crepe

Crunchy Cookies

Delish French Toast Sticks

Shamrock Shake

**Lean & Green Meal:**

Spinach Haddock Fillets

Broccoli Waffles

**Snack:**

4 ounces grapefruit

**DAY 5**

**Fueling Hacks:**

Pumpkin Frappe

No Bake Chocolate Haystacks

Eggnog

Marshmallow Cereal Treat

**Lean & Green Meal:**

Salmon Soup

Italian Shrimp Meal

**Snack:**

¾ cup low-fat plain yogurt

## DAY 6

**Fueling Hacks:**

Berry Mojito

Vanilla Shake

Mint Cookies

Mocha Cake

**Lean & Green Meal:**

Turkey Soup

Taco Broccoli Bowl

**Snack:**

½ cup fresh blueberries

## DAY 7

**Fueling Hacks:**

Chocolate Donuts

Chicken Nuggets

Pizza Bites

Chocolate Popsicles

**Lean & Green Meal:**

Salmon Lettuce Wraps

Lemon Chicken

**Snack:**

1 cup unsweetened almond milk

## Week 3

### DAY 1

**Fueling Hacks:**

Vanilla Shake

Mocha Cake

Pumpkin Waffles

Chicken Nuggets

**Lean & Green Meal**

Salmon Soup

Stuffed Chicken

**Snack:**

½ cup canned peaches (packed in water or natural juices)

### DAY 2

**Fueling Hacks:**

Pumpkin Frappe

Pizza Bites

Mint Cookies

Delish French Toast Sticks

**Lean & Green Meal:**

**Snack:**

¾ cup low-fat plain yogurt

## DAY 3

**Fueling Hacks:**

Eggnog

Maple Pancakes

Little Fudge Balls

Brownie Cookies

**Lean & Green Meal:**

High-Protein Salad

Zucchini Haddock Fillets

**Snack:**

½ cup fresh strawberries

## DAY 4

**Fueling Hacks:**

Pumpkin Frappe

Marshmallow Cereal Treat

Crunchy Cookies

Brownie Pudding Cups

**Lean & Green Meal:**

Turkey Soup

Seafood Feast

**Snack:**

½ ounce pistachios

**DAY 5**

**Fueling Hacks:**

Eggnog

Chicken Nuggets

Richly Tasty Crepe

Maple Pancakes

**Lean & Green Meal:**

Chicken Soup

Asian Style Beef

**Snack:**

1 cup unsweetened cashew milk

**DAY 6**

**Fueling Hacks:**

Pumpkin Frappe

Chocolate Donuts

Pumpkin Waffles

Mint Cookies

**Lean & Green Meal:**

Beef Soup

Spinach Haddock Fillets

**Snack:**

2 Dill Pickle Spears

**DAY 7**

**Fueling Hacks:**

Vanilla Shake

Mocha Cake

Pizza Bites

Maple Pancakes

Tropical Smoothie Bowl

**Lean & Green Meal:**

Salmon Salad

Lemon Chicken

**Snack:**

4 ounces orange

# Week 4

**DAY 1**

**Fueling Hacks:**

Berry Mojito

Crunchy Cookies

Delish French Toast Sticks

Little Fudge Balls

**Lean & Green Meal:**

Sirloin Steak Soup

Seafood Feast

**Snack:**

1 cup unsweetened almond milk

**DAY 2**

**Fueling Hacks:**

Shamrock Shake

Chicken Nuggets

Mint Cookies

Maple Pancakes

**Lean & Green Meal:**

Taco Broccoli Bowl

Italian Shrimp

**Snack:**

3 celery stalks

**DAY 3**

**Fueling Hacks:**

Pumpkin Frappe

Pizza Bites

Brownie Cookies

Chocolate Popsicles

**Lean & Green Meal:**

Vegetable Curry

Chicken Fajita Platter

**Snack:**

¾ cup low-fat plain yogurt

**DAY 4**

**Fueling Hacks:**

Shamrock Shake

Little Fudge Balls

Richly Tasty Crepe

Mint Cookies

**Lean & Green Meal:**

Herbed Chicken

Pan-Seared Scallops

**Snack:**

½ ounce almonds

**DAY 5**

**Fueling Hacks:**

Berry Mojito

Mint Cookies

Maple Pancakes

Mocha Cake

**Lean & Green Meal:**

Green Beans Soup

Zucchini Halibut

**Snack:**

4 ounces grapefruit

**DAY 6**

**Fueling Hacks:**

Pumpkin Frappe

Mocha Cake

Pumpkin Waffles

Delish French Toast Sticks

**Lean & Green Meal:**

Asian style Beef

Avocado Chicken Salad

**Snack:**

½ ounce cashews

**DAY 7**

**Fueling Hacks:**

Berry Mojito

Chocolate Donuts

Pizza Bites

Crunchy Cookies

**Lean & Green Meal:**

Tofu Soup

Stuffed Chicken

**Snack:**

½ cup fresh blueberries

# Conclusion

The Lean & Green diet plan is a healthy approach towards an effective weight loss and nutritious lifestyle. It contains cooked proteins (5-7 oz.), 3 servings of non-starchy veggies, and 2 servings of healthy fats. You can have six meals a day, i.e., both Lean & Green meals & Fuelings. Moreover, you can adjust your eating routine according to your daily routine, empowering you to make decisions towards a healthy lifestyle.

Made in the USA
Columbia, SC
26 April 2021